Tucholsky Wagner Zola Scott Sydow Freud Schlegel
Turgenev Wallace Fonatne
Twain Walther von der Vogelweide Fouqué Friedrich II. von Preußen
Weber Freiligrath
Kant Ernst Frey
Fechner Fichte Weiße Rose von Fallersleben Richthofen Frommel
Hölderlin
Engels Fielding Eichendorff Tacitus Dumas
Fehrs Faber Flaubert
Eliasberg Ebner Eschenbach
Maximilian I. von Habsburg Fock Zweig
Feuerbach Eliot
Ewald Vergil
Goethe London
Elisabeth von Österreich
Mendelssohn Balzac Shakespeare Dostojewski Ganghofer
Lichtenberg Rathenau Doyle Gjellerup
Trackl Stevenson Hambruch
Tolstoi Lenz Droste-Hülshoff
Mommsen Hanrieder
Thoma von Arnim Hägele Humboldt
Dach Verne Hauff
Reuter Rousseau Hagen Hauptmann Gautier
Karrillon Garschin
Defoe Baudelaire
Damaschke Hebbel
Descartes Hegel Kussmaul Herder
Wolfram von Eschenbach Schopenhauer
Dickens Rilke George
Bronner Darwin Melville Grimm Jerome
Bebel Proust
Campe Horváth Aristoteles
Voltaire Federer
Bismarck Vigny Barlach Herodot
Gengenbach Heine
Storm Casanova Tersteegen Gilm Grillparzer Georgy
Chamberlain Lessing Langbein Gryphius
Brentano Lafontaine
Strachwitz Claudius Schiller Kralik Iffland Sokrates
Bellamy Schilling
Katharina II. von Rußland Gerstäcker Raabe Gibbon Tschechow
Löns Hesse Hoffmann Gogol Wilde Vulpius
Gleim
Luther Heym Hofmannsthal Morgenstern
Klee Hölty Goedicke
Roth Heyse Klopstock Kleist
Luxemburg Puschkin Homer Mörike Musil
Machiavelli La Roche Horaz
Navarra Aurel Musset Kierkegaard Kraft Kraus
Lamprecht Kind Hugo Moltke
Nestroy Marie de France Kirchhoff
Laotse Ipsen Liebknecht
Nietzsche Nansen Ringelnatz
Marx Lassalle Gorki Klett Leibniz
von Ossietzky May vom Stein Lawrence Irving
Petalozzi Knigge
Platon Pückler Michelangelo Kafka
Sachs Poe Kock
Liebermann Korolenko
de Sade Praetorius Mistral Zetkin

The publishing house tredition has created the series **TREDITION CLASSICS**. It contains classical literature works from over two thousand years. Most of these titles have been out of print and off the bookstore shelves for decades.

The book series is intended to preserve the cultural legacy and to promote the timeless works of classical literature. As a reader of a **TREDITION CLASSICS** book, the reader supports the mission to save many of the amazing works of world literature from oblivion.

The symbol of **TREDITION CLASSICS** is Johannes Gutenberg (1400 – 1468), the inventor of movable type printing.

With the series, tredition intends to make thousands of international literature classics available in printed format again – worldwide.

All books are available at book retailers worldwide in paperback and in hard-cover. For more information please visit: www.tredition.com

tredition was established in 2006 by Sandra Latusseck and Soenke Schulz. Based in Hamburg, Germany, tredition offers publishing solutions to authors and publishing houses, combined with worldwide distribution of printed and digital book content. tredition is uniquely positioned to enable authors and publishing houses to create books on their own terms and without conventional manufacturing risks.

For more information please visit: www.tredition.com

Studies in the Life of the Christian

Henry T. (Henry Thorne) Sell

Imprint

This book is part of the TREDITION CLASSICS series.

Author: Henry T. (Henry Thorne) Sell
Cover design: toepferschumann, Berlin (Germany)

Publisher: tredition GmbH, Hamburg (Germany)
ISBN: 978-3-8495-0753-4

www.tredition.com
www.tredition.de

PREFACE

These studies consider the questions: What did Christ teach? What is the standpoint of Christianity? What is a Christian? What ought he to believe and why? How shall he regard the Bible and the church? What should be his relations to God, to his fellow men, to his home, to society, to business, and to the state?

The strength and reasonableness of the great main positions of Christian faith and service are constructively presented. Careful attention is also given to the practical application of Christian principles to the perplexing problems of modern life.

This book is for use in adult Bible classes, Bible study circles, pastors' training classes in the essentials of Christianity, educational institutions and private study.

It is uniform with the author's "Bible Studies in the Life of Christ," "Bible Studies in the Life of Paul" and his other Bible study books.

HENRY T. SELL.
Chicago.

CONTENTS

I. CHRIST, THE GREAT TEACHER

II. THE CHRISTIAN'S GOD

III. THE CHRISTIAN MAN

IV. THE CHRISTIAN'S FELLOW MAN

V. THE CHRISTIAN FAITH

VI. THE CHRISTIAN'S BOOK

VII. THE CHRISTIAN PRAYER

VIII. THE CHRISTIAN SERVICE

IX. THE CHRISTIAN CHURCH

X. THE CHRISTIAN HOME

XI. THE CHRISTIAN BUSINESS WORLD

XII. THE CHRISTIAN SOCIETY

XIII. THE CHRISTIAN STATE

XIV. THE CHRISTIAN'S HOPE

STUDY I

CHRIST, THE GREAT TEACHER

Scripture references: Matthew 4:23; 5:1,2; 7:29; 13:54; 26:55; 28:19,20; Mark 1:21,22; 4:1,2; 6:6; Luke 5:3; 11:1; 19:47; John 6:59; 7:14; 8:28.

THE FOUNDER OF CHRISTIANITY

The heart of the Christian religion is found in Jesus Christ. If we desire to know what Christianity is and of what elements it is composed we must look to Him and His teachings. He is the great source of our knowledge of what God, man, sin, righteousness, duty and salvation are.

Our interest in the books of the Old Testament lies in the fact that they lead up to Him. We study the books of the New Testament because of their vivid portrayal of His life, teachings, death and resurrection. With Jesus Christ a new era dawned for the world with new principles, ideas and aspirations for humanity. His teachings touch every department of human life and, where they are accepted and followed, they show their marvellous transforming power. There can be no more important study than what Jesus Christ said and did while upon this earth. "Never man spake like this man" (John 7:46).

WHAT CHRIST TAUGHT

There are five great lines which His teachings followed; they have to do with God, man, sin, salvation and the future life.

The Right Relation of God to Man and Man to God. — How does God regard man? and, How shall man look upon God? are questions upon which the best thought of men in all ages has been expended. Upon the answers given have been founded all sorts of religious and philosophical systems.

Man in this great universe desires to know in what relation he stands to the Author of it. Is man only a creature of fate? What does God care, great as He is, for one man?

Jesus Christ recognized this desire of man to know his standing with God and He proclaimed not only the power, but the Fatherhood of God. When He taught His disciples how to pray He began His immortal prayer not with "Great God of the universe," or "Creator of all things," but "After this manner therefore pray ye: Our Father which art in heaven" (Matthew 6:9). Here was a new conception of God.

Through Christ man comes into personal relations with God as the Father (John 16:27) who cares for him as a son. Man is to love and forgive as God loves and forgives in this relation of Father (Matthew 22:37; 6:14,15). Man is to do all that he does as in the sight of his Father in heaven (Matthew 6:1-26). God is made known as supreme love (John 3:16).

The Right Relation of Man to Man. — There are many causes which divide men into classes, castes and nationalities. Once divided men begin to develop a class feeling and pride which tend to deepen and widen the gulfs which separate them from each other.

With the truth proclaimed by Christ of the "Fatherhood of God" came also the great truth of the "Brotherhood of Man." The true relation of man to man, no matter what the caste, class, employment or nationality, is that of sons who have a common father. The second great commandment given by Christ is, "Thou shalt love thy neighbour as thyself" (Matthew 22:39). When He took the example for a good neighbour He selected a Samaritan, a man of an alien race. Men are naturally inclined to do good to those who treat them well and whose help they need; but Christ, in carrying out this new law of brotherly love said, "Love your enemies, bless them that curse you, do good to them that hate you, and pray for them which despitefully use you, and persecute you, that ye may be the children of your Father which is in heaven" (Matthew 5:44-48). It is only through this love of man for man, no matter what the class or condition, that right relations between men can ever be established and maintained.

The Right Relation of Man to Sin.—Man violates his sense of righteousness and justice. He transgresses the laws of God and his nature. Man's sin is everywhere doing its destroying work. There is individual, social, corporate and national sin (Romans 3:23). This fact of sin is not only set forth in the Bible in unmistakable terms, but every government recognizes it in its laws and courts of justice. Society puts up its bars to protect itself against the sinner, and all literature proclaims the evil results of sin.

What ought to be man's attitude to sin? Shall he make light of it and call it a necessary part of living? Shall he continue in it, although he recognizes its evil results, and draw others with him into greater and larger violations of the laws of God and man? These are practical questions. Some temporize with sin and say, "Let us lead outwardly correct lives, but within certain bounds we will do as we please"; hence arises the practice of secret sinning.

Christ came declaring that man's relation to sin should be uncompromising. He used vigorous language in regard to sin. He said, "Woe unto the world because of offenses! for it must needs be that offenses come; but woe to that man by whom the offense cometh! Wherefore if thy hand or thy foot offend thee, cut them off and cast them from thee: it is better for thee to enter into life halt or maimed, rather than having two hands or feet to be cast into everlasting fire" (Matthew 18:7,8). But Jesus in thus advocating heroic treatment for sin was but doing what eminent surgeons are advising every day in regard to certain dangerous bodily diseases. Jesus also laid His finger on the source of sin when He declared, "For out of the heart proceed evil thoughts, murders, adulteries, fornications, thefts, false witness, blasphemies: these are the things which defile a man" (Matthew 15:19). A man must think evil before he does evil, and hence the emphasis which Jesus placed upon keeping the heart clean.

The Right Relation of Man to Salvation.—Man feels his inclination to do evil and, seeing also the degradation wrought by it, desires to be saved from it. The cry has gone up from many hearts to be free not only from the power of sin but from the desire to commit sin. No man can save himself. He may succeed in a certain outward reformation and correctness of habit and speech, but he cannot control the thoughts and inclinations of his own heart.

The special mission of Jesus Christ was to place man in the right relation of salvation from his sins and to show Himself the Saviour of Man. It was declared of Him before His birth, "He shall save His people from their sins" (Matthew 1:21). He said at the last supper, "This is My blood of the New Testament which is shed for many for the remission of sins" (Matthew 26:28). He had power to forgive sins (Mark 2:10). He said not, "I show you the way," but "I am the way, the truth and the life" (John 14:6). There is here a mighty spiritual power which can save man from sin and can keep him from the desire to sin. It is only as man enters into personal relations with Jesus Christ, repenting of his sin and having faith in Him, that the burden of sin is lifted from his heart (Matthew 6:33; 11:28,30).

The Right Relation of Man to Death and the Future Life.—The facts of death and of what comes after cannot be set aside; they must be faced. All forms of religion and systems of philosophy have striven to sustain and comfort men at their trying hour of need. The trouble has been, however, to find any certain ground of the hope of a future life upon which to rest. No man has been able to do more than present a good argument, in regard to the hereafter, which might or might not be true.

But when Jesus Christ came He was able to speak with authority and power. He plainly, in His description of the last judgment scene (Matthew 25:31-46), showed the relation of man's faith and actions in this world to his state in the world to come. He declared that a man need have no fear of death or the hereafter who trusted in Him. "I am the resurrection, and the life: he that believeth in Me, though he were dead yet shall he live: and whosoever liveth and believeth in Me shall never die" (John 11:25,26). "In My Father's house are many mansions, if it were not so I would have told you. I go to prepare a place for you" (John 14:2). In a supreme trust in Jesus Christ all dread of death and the hereafter may be taken away and man may enter into a right relation to immortality in this life.

FORMS OF CHRIST'S TEACHING

He used many forms in placing the truth before men. He paid great regard to the timeliness and the manner of presenting what He had to teach. Upon many occasions the multitudes were so captivated by His words and works that they followed Him out into desert places.

Direct Discourse. — The Sermon on the Mount is a good example of this teaching. Here He taught plainly, (1) "The nature and constitution of the Kingdom" (Matthew 5:1-16); in itself (blessedness, vs. 1-12) and in its relation to the world (vs. 13-16). (2) The law of the kingdom (Matthew 5:17-7:12); general principles (vs. 17-20), the moral law (vs. 21-48), religious duty (6:1-18), and duty in relation to the world and the good and evil things in it (6: 19-7:12). (3) Invitations to enter the kingdom (Matthew 7:13-29).

He was equally plain in regard to His own mission. He declared Himself to be the Son of God and claimed equality with the Father (John 5:18-23). He said, "I and My Father are one" (John 10:30). He affirmed His preexistence and that He had glory with the Father before the world was (John 17:5) and whoever had seen Him had seen the Father (John 14:9). At His trial, in answer to the question of the High Priest, He declared that He was the Christ, the Son of God (Matthew 26:63-66). After His resurrection He told His disciples, in sending them forth to their mission, that all power was given Him in heaven and in earth (Matthew 28:18-20).

Parables (Mark 4:2; Matthew 13:3). — Christ spoke in parables to convey and send home to the hearts of His hearers the truth, just as Nathan employed the parable of the lamb in the case of David to make him acknowledge his sin. They were adapted to the capacities of His hearers. Each parable had some great central truth.

The parables have been classified as:

1. The Theoretic, which teach general truths concerning the kingdom of God, such as, "The Sower" (Matthew 13:3-23), "The Treasure" and "The Pearl" (Matthew 13:44,45).

2. Grace, setting forth the divine goodness and grace as the source of salvation and law of Christian life, such as, "The Lost Coin," "The Lost Sheep" and "The Lost Boy" (Luke 15).

3. The Prophetic or Judgment parables, which proclaim the righteousness of God as the supreme ruler, rewarding men according to their works, such as, "The Wicked Husbandmen" (Matthew 21:33-41), and "The Ten Virgins" (Matthew 25:1-13).

Miracles (John 3:2; 2:23; 6:2; Mark 1:32-34).—Christ appealed to His works as an evidence of His divine mission (John 10:38). Miracles are possible, probable and credible, when we believe there is a personal God, who is the Supreme Ruler of the universe and that He cares for man.

The thirty-six miracles of which an account is given in the four gospels have been divided into three classes; their teaching is important:

1. The Nature miracles show the divinity of Christ. The feeding of the five thousand men (Matthew 14:15-21) reveals His creative power, and the stilling of the storm on the Lake of Galilee (Matthew 8:23-27) His divine command over Nature and its forces.

2. The Healing miracles reveal not only His divinity but His humanity and compassion. They set forth the one being who loves the human race with His whole heart. This class of miracles shows the mission of Jesus to be the extinction of sin and disease, and the redemption of man, body and soul.

3. The Moral miracles are the life of Christ and its effect upon the world.

Example of Living and Dying, the teaching of which is elaborated in the Acts and Epistles (Acts 1:8; 2:31-41; 13:23-42; Philippians 2:5-11; Colossians 1:13-20).

HOW CHRIST TAUGHT

With Authority (Matthew 7:28,29; Mark 1:22).—He declared that "All power is given unto Me in heaven and in earth" (Matthew 28:18). He did not quote precedents but said, "I say unto you."

With Persuasiveness and Love (Matthew 11:28-30; 19:13,14; John 3:17; Luke 9:56).—People of all classes gathered about Him, in the marketplaces, in the fields and by the seaside. They followed Him into desert places to hear the gracious words that fell from His lips.

With Originality (John 12:46). — He taught a new philosophy of sorrow and suffering, a new law of self-sacrifice and a new law of love for fallen humanity.

With Promise (Matthew 28:20; John 14:12-19; 16:1-14; Acts 1:4-8). — His work He declared was not to end with His resurrection and ascension, but was to continue. He promised to endue His disciples with power from on high in their task of converting a world. This promise of divine help was also extended to all His disciples in their effort to lead pure and righteous lives.

QUESTIONS

What can be said about the Founder of Christianity and His teachings? What did Christ teach; about the right relation of God to man, man to man, man to sin, man to salvation and man to death and the hereafter? What can be said of the forms of Christ's teaching; direct discourse (give examples), parables (give the teaching of the three classes), miracles (give the teaching of the three classes) and example of living and dying? How did Christ teach? What can be said of His authority, persuasiveness, originality and promise?

STUDY II

THE CHRISTIAN'S GOD

Scripture References: Genesis 1:1; 17:1; Exodus 34:6,7; 20:3-7; Deuteronomy 32:4; 33:27; Isaiah 40:28; 45:21; Psalm 90:2; 145:17; 139:1-12; John 1:1-5; 1:18; 4:23,24; 14:6-11; Matthew 28:19,20; Revelation 4:11; 22:13.

WHO IS GOD?

How Shall We Think of God?—"Upon the conception that is entertained of God will depend the nature and quality of the religion of any soul or race; and in accordance with the view that is held of God, His nature, His character and His relation to other beings, the spirit and the substance of theology will be determined." When one man says, "I believe in God" he may have in mind an entirely different conception of God from another man who uses the same expression. There is a Christian idea of God and there are many non-Christian ideas about God; it is the latter which keep men from heartily engaging in the service of the Lord Jesus Christ.

Wrong Conceptions of God.—Some of these are:

1. That He is a blind fate or unknowable force. Personality is denied, and it is asserted that this great force neither sees, cares nor even knows what men do or do not do.

2. Even if this great force be personal, and knows what is going on amongst men, He is perfectly indifferent to right or wrong actions.

3. God knows and sees all that is going on, but He has wound up this universe like a great clock. To help or succour any man in his distress would disarrange the whole system. Natural law must have its course; it is useless to pray.

4. God is revengeful or weak; in the first place men seek to keep out of His way, in the second they do not care.

When men adopt these wrong ideas of God and cherish them they are fashioned after them in life and character. Here are the stumbling-blocks which need to be removed before men, who think this way, can be brought into sympathy with the Church of Christ. Man can never come into personal loving relations with a Universal Substance or Force, no matter how mighty it is.

Right Conceptions of God are necessary for the true worship of the Almighty, for the exercise of proper conduct to our fellow men and for the upbuilding of our own spiritual life. Never was there a time when the great fundamental positions of the Bible, in regard to God, needed to be more plainly stated than to-day. When men stand firmly upon these positions a whole host of perplexities and anxieties will take their departure.

The Christian Conception of God has been thus expressed, "God is the Personal Spirit, perfectly good, who in holy love, creates, sustains and orders all." The essential matters covered in this statement are:

1. The nature of God. He is the Personal Spirit (Exodus 3:14; John 4:24) who can enter into personal relations with man, and who hears and answers prayer.

2. The character of God. He is perfectly good, pure and holy (Psalm 25:8; Nahum 1:7; Romans 2:4). Man may have perfect confidence, however matters may seem to him to go wrong with his imperfect vision of the world and the happenings in it, that there is a good God who governs all in the interest of righteousness (Matthew 13:24-30,36-43).

3. The relation of God to all other existences. He creates, sustains and orders all (Genesis 1:1; Psalm 19).

4. The motive of God in His relation to all other existence; it is holy love (1 John 4:8).

Supreme power, personality, intelligence and perfect goodness are then the great revealed truths which the Bible presents to us as the proper conceptions which we should have of God.

But if it is desired to know what God is like we look at once to Jesus Christ. He is supreme intelligence. He has power over nature and men and He uses all with the motive and purpose of a holy love. We know that He controlled nature, when on earth, and not nature Him. He taught the great love of God for man. He made it plain that men were not in a relation as atoms of matter in a whirlpool of action, but as sons to a loving father.

GOD IS SUPREME

God's Attitude to the Universe.—The Scriptures are consistent in the statement, many times made, that God is the source of all things. He brings all things into being and sustains all by the word of His power. His is a work of perpetual administration. But God is not wholly occupied in conducting the affairs of the universe, neither does it exhaust His possibilities (Psalm 8:1; 148:13). He is greater than the universe. God, says Dr. Clarke, in his "Outline of Christian Theology," is like the spirit of a man in his body, which is greater than his body, able to direct his body, and capable of activities that far transcend the physical realm. God is a free spirit, personal, self-directing, unexhausted by His present activities. This statement affirms both the immanence and the transcendence of God. By the immanence of God is meant that He is everywhere and always present in the universe, nowhere absent from it, never separated from its life. By His transcendence is meant—not as is sometimes represented—that He is outside and views the universe from beyond and above, but that He is not shut up in it or limited by it, not required in His totality to maintain and order it. By both together is meant that He is a free spirit inhabiting the universe, but surpassing it, immanent as always in the universe, and transcendent, as always independent of its limitations and able to act upon it.

God's Attitude to Man.—God has not only placed man at the head of the animal world, but has endowed him with qualities which make him its lord and master. God is more than the Creator of man. He is his Father, Saviour and Friend.

God comes to man in the attitude, of The Supreme Spiritual Being, approaching a spiritual being who is of priceless value. Jesus

Christ makes this truth very plain. He everywhere teaches the great worth of the life of a man and that God is seeking to come directly into touch with this life which is so precious in His sight (John 3:16; Matthew 10:30,31). This life is not the physical but the spiritual which is the real life of a man. "Not what one has, but what one is, gives the true measure of a man." He said, "For what shall it profit a man, if he shall gain the whole world and lose his own soul? Or what shall a man give in exchange for his soul?" (Mark 8:36,37). "Is not the life more than meat and the body than raiment?" (Matthew 6:25). "In harmony with this view of the worth of life," Professor Stevens in "The Theology of the New Testament," says, "Jesus taught that the most humble and insignificant person, on whom men set no value, is precious in the sight of God. These little ones, be they children or humble believers, are not the despised (Matthew 18:10). The least important person who goes astray from goodness excites the pity and solicitude of God, and He seeks him and brings him back as the shepherd, leaving his ninety-nine sheep, goes into the mountains in eager search after the one that has wandered away" (Luke 15:14).

The hope of everlasting life is bound up with the recognition by man of the priceless value of the spiritual life and of the necessity of his coming into harmony (in thought, will and action) with God's plans for him (John 17:3; Luke 12:16-21; John 1:4; 3:15,34-36; 6:35,47; 14:6).

"GOD IS THE PERSONAL SPIRIT"

"God is Spirit," these words of Christ, uttered to the Samaritan woman (John 4:24), have reference to the nature of God and show us how we are to think of Him. He is not limited to a particular place of worship, but is to be worshipped "in spirit and in truth" (John 4:23).

When we speak of a spirit we mean a being who has intelligence and will; one who thinks, feels and wills. God the great intelligence and will can enter into communication with man who, while he has a body, has also a spirit possessing intelligence and a will. We need not define the difference between God and matter, "if only we give full weight to this vital and practical difference, that He is one who thinks and feels and wills. The composition of spirit we may never understand, but this is the action of spirit and this is intelligible." God is everywhere represented in the Scriptures as exercising intelligence and will (Genesis 1:1,2; 6:3; Job 26:7-14; 38:1-41; Psalm 2; 19; 72; Isaiah 61:1; Mark 10:27; 12:27; John 3:34; Acts 3:26).

God is Personal.—Personality has two characteristics; self-consciousness and self-direction. When it is said that God is personal, the meaning is that He knows Himself as God and directs His own actions. In the Bible He is represented as saying "I" (Exodus 20:2; 3:14) and as directing all things. Personality does not limit God. He is the one perfect personality. Personality in man exists only in a more or less imperfect degree. Personality is understood here not as "bodily," but as belonging to the spirit.

GOD IS GOOD

The Character of God is a subject of great importance to man. God is the Supreme Personal Spirit, yet to know only this is to leave out a very vital part in our estimation or knowledge of God. We desire to know and feel that God is not only the greatest, but the best being in the universe. Hence God is shown to us in the Bible to be inwardly perfect and outwardly consistent with this perfection. The Old Testament shows a struggle between God and man; God seeking to bring man to the thinking of right thoughts and doing of right actions and man resisting Him. The history of Israel is a story of a nation whom God would make a righteous people; all the laws given to it, civil, sanitary and ceremonial, were with the end in view to make it "a holy nation"; all its prophets and teachers proclaim the righteous and just character of God (Exodus 19:6; Leviticus 11:45; 19:2; 20:7, 8; Numbers 15:40; Deuteronomy 14:2,21; Joshua 24:19; Psalm 22:3; 99:3; 111:9; Isaiah 6:3; 57:15). In Jesus Christ and His life upon earth we see the goodness of God in its largeness. "In His gospel holiness is the ideal, the substance of Christian character and the end in view in Christian experience." He says, in the Sermon on the Mount, "Be ye therefore perfect, even as your Father which is in heaven is perfect" (Matthew 5:48).

In Christ we have the one perfect ideal of moral excellence. In Him we can see what goodness in God means (John 14:9).

The standard for the conduct of man is that of God's goodness, righteousness and truth; this is not a double one — the Old and the New Testament — but a single one and applicable to all men of all races and climes.

"If sin exists holiness in God must absolutely and forever oppose it. From the holiness in God's character we can understand His righteousness and justice. The man who does evil sets his will against God's will and against the principle upon which He conducts the universe. Such a man has placed himself where he must either turn back and forsake his sin or take the inevitable consequences of resisting the purpose which God is fulfilling."

God's love for man is bound up with His goodness. God, foreseeing the fearful consequences of man's sinning, seeks in every way to warn and turn him back from the evil way. He knows the great worth of the soul and desires to save it to everlasting joy (John 3:17; Luke 9:56; John 14:1-3).

GOD'S MANIFESTATION

The Manifestation of God in Jesus Christ. — Paul says, "when the fullness of time was come, God sent forth His Son" (Galatians 4:4); "That at the name of Jesus every knee should bow, of things in heaven, and things in earth, and things under the earth; and that every tongue should confess that Jesus Christ is Lord to the glory of God the Father" (Philippians 2:10,11).

This personal manifestation of God in Christ is in perfect harmony with the nature and character of God as we know Him through the Scriptures. This manifestation of God is not only subject to a historical test, but may also be made the subject of a personal experience test, "If any man will do His will he shall know of the doctrine" (John 7:17). Soon after the resurrection and ascension of Jesus the disciples, who had been with Jesus when He was upon earth, began to urge others to make a test of personal experience in regard to the manifestation of God in Christ (Acts 2:14,31-47; 3:19-21; 7:56).

Paul, who had a special experience (Acts 9:1-8), preached this test of personal experience throughout the Roman Empire. Ever since those early times there has been the same urgent appeal for men to come to a knowledge of God through Jesus Christ and to make the test not only historical, but one of personal experience.

The "Threefold Self-manifestation of God."—Christ in instructing His disciples after His resurrection, said, "Go ye therefore and teach all nations, baptizing them in the name of the Father and of the Son and of the Holy Ghost" (Matthew 28:19).

In the Old Testament we have the manifestation of God as the one living God of all. He was specially known as the God of Israel in preparing that nation for the great part it had in the divine economy.

In the New Testament Christ is recognized by His followers—and so taught Himself—as the personal manifestation of God, to whom divine honour was and is to be given. Christ told His followers that He would "pray the Father and He shall give you another Comforter, that He may abide with you forever" (John 14:16). This Comforter (16:7-15), the Holy Spirit, would guide them into all truth.

The Holy Spirit, upon whom they were to wait for His manifestation (Acts 1:8), came in wonderful power on the Day of Pentecost (Acts 2:1-4), thus beginning the great work which was to spread around the world. When Paul and Barnabas were ready for their large missionary task, the Holy Spirit called them to it (Acts 13:2). The early Church felt the presence of that mighty indwelling Holy Spirit. "As God Himself had come in the Son so it was felt that He had come in the Spirit. The one God of all known to the fathers, had manifested Himself in the divine human Christ, and in the invisible Spirit of truth and life. Both was His and yet each was truly Himself."

QUESTIONS

Who is God? How shall we think of Him? Give some of the wrong conceptions of God. What can be said of the right conceptions of God? What is the Christian conception of God? How can we know what God is like? What is God's attitude to the universe and to man? What do we mean when we say, that "God is a Spirit"? How is God personal? What can be said of the character of God? How is God manifested, in Christ, and in the threefold manifestation?

STUDY III

THE CHRISTIAN MAN

Scripture references: Genesis 1:26-28; 2:7; 9:6; Job 33:4; Psalm 100:3; 8:4-9; Ecclesiastes 7:29; Acts 17:26-28; 1 Corinthians 11:7; Ephesians 4:24; Colossians 3:10; 1 Corinthians 15:45; Hebrews 2:6,7; Ephesians 6:10-18; 1 Corinthians 2:9.

WHAT IS MAN?

What Shall We Think of Man?—Who is he? What is his place on the earth and in the universe? What is his destiny? He is of necessity an object of thought. He is the subject of natural laws, instincts and passions. How far is he free; how far bound? How is he linked with the physical and the spiritual worlds? These and a host of other questions press upon us for answers, when we begin to think about man and his destiny.

Taken in detail the inquiries lead investigators in many different directions and result in many contradictory systems of thought. Taken, however, in a general practical way all questions about man may be considered from two standpoints; the physical and the spiritual. The danger is in making the physical alone interpret the spiritual and in declaring that "man is simply a ripple on the sea of human events and human life, merely on episode marking a particular stage in the cooling of a nebula." This method of interpretation leads to the ruling out of any personal responsibility on the part of man for his thoughts or actions, the obliteration of the distinction between right and wrong and the denial of a personal God and personal immortality.

The right standpoint from which to consider the many questions about man, as he appears upon this earth, is that of a personal spiritual being with a physical body. There is here no denial of the physical part of man, but it is made subordinate to the spiritual. Man is personal and responsible for his thoughts and conduct; upon this conception of man is founded human society and the state. Man is spiritual, knowing the distinction between right and wrong, capable of knowing God who is The Personal Spirit and looking forward to a personal immortality.

The Christian Thought of Man recognizes him as a personal spiritual being with a physical body; he has large responsibilities, and a great destiny to attain—if he so wills.

There are six heads under which the Christian conception of man may be considered:

1. Man is mortal (Psalm 90:5,10; Ecclesiastes 12:5). The physical part of man is quite definitely limited in years. His body is formed of the same elements as that of any other animal and is subject to the law of decay and death. This linking of man with, what we call, the material universe is asserted at the very opening of the Bible (Genesis 2:7). Man is a member of a race of men with all that this membership implies (Acts 17:26).

2. Man is immortal (1 Corinthians 15:53,54). The physical body is the house of the spirit of man. All the appeals in the Scriptures are addressed to this personal spirit of man (Matthew 6:25,33; John 14:1-4). There is in the New Testament a great forward look to the things that shall come to pass after the passing away of the physical body (Matthew 25:31-46; Revelation 21,22).

3. Man is a moral being (Romans 2:14,15). There is a law of conscience impressed upon man when he comes into the world, which makes him a moral being capable of distinguishing between right and wrong. Man knows when he sins against the law of his conscience.

4. Man is a responsible being (Romans 2:1-11). He is self-conscious and self-determining. He knows himself as himself and he can determine his actions; it is these characteristics which make him responsible for his sins. He has the power of choice and in willing to do right or wrong he brings the consequences of his doing upon himself.

5. Salvation for man is through Jesus Christ. Man sins and violates his moral nature; he feels the responsibility for his sin; he desires forgiveness for his sin and to be freed from its power over his spiritual nature (Romans 7:23,24). But he finds no earthly help. Such help can come to man only through a spiritual being who, subject to all the assaults of sin (Matthew 4:1-11), has triumphed over them all (Romans 8:1-4; 2 Corinthians 5:21). Jesus Christ, the manifestation of God the Father, is the Spiritual Being through whom man can receive forgiveness for sin (Luke 5:23,24; Acts 2:38; 13:38,39; 16:30,31).

6. Large possibilities are everywhere asserted for man in the Scriptures. This earthly life is looked upon as the beginning of a greater and fuller life (1 Corinthians 13:9,12). Yet in doing the will of God man may even here enter upon a life full of joy (Hebrews 12:1,2).

MAN MADE IN THE IMAGE OF GOD

The Statement of the Case. — In Genesis 1:26 we are told that God said, "Let us make man in our image, after our likeness." In Genesis 2:7 the narrative relates, "And the Lord God formed man of the dust of the ground and breathed into his nostrils the breath of life and man became a living soul" (see Psalm 8:4-8). These passages have a great representative character and the truth expressed in them has lived and will live under all theories of the appearance of man upon this earth. In the Bible man is shown as the latest and highest creation of God, the last and best of His work in the animal world, but with a difference that is world-wide between him and the brute creation. Here is an animal, coming up out of the dust, endowed with spiritual qualities which place him not only at the head of the animal kingdom, but dominating it. The most radical evolutionist must admit that man is the last in the list of uplifts in the animal world, that he has qualities which elevate him far above it and by which he dominates it. Somewhere back there, again, he must admit that there came a change and the dust-born animal was changed into a God-born soul. The great truth then remains, man is an animal but endowed with a growing marvellous self-conscious, self-determining personality. As the Bible is a progressive revelation, showing us more and more the greatness of spiritual truths, it represents man as starting from no high plane of civilization and as a learner through the ages. Man is even now in the process of making; he has not yet come to his best estate.

The Image of God.—What is the likeness of God? "God is Spirit" (John 4:24) and that part of man which counts is his spiritual kinship to God.

Man's intelligence, moral nature and will constitute "the image of God" in him and make it possible for him to come into communication with God and to occupy his unique place in the universe. Only a person can understand a person.

"Man is dear to God because he is like Him. Vast and glorious as it is, the sun cannot think God's thoughts; can fulfill but cannot intelligently sympathize with God's purposes. Man, alone among God's works, can enter into and approve of God's purpose in the world and can intelligently fulfill it. Without man the whole material universe would have been dark and unintelligible, mechanical and apparently without any sufficient purpose. Matter, however fearfully and wonderfully wrought, is but the platform and material in which spirit, intelligence and will, may fulfill themselves and find development."

The Bible seeks to show men in how many ways they resemble God and to urge them to be worthy of their likeness to God. There is a certain philosophy on the other hand, sometimes called "the dirt philosophy," which seeks to show men in how many ways they resemble the brute and to urge them to live the life of the brute.

But a great practical question which demands an answer of us—as we look out upon the world of men taking them as they are—is, Did God make the evil man "in His likeness" as well as the good man?

The Good Man.—The best things bear the stamp of their maker. If a good judge of pictures is taken into some famous art gallery it is not necessary to point out to him the excellencies of the paintings, they tell their own story. There are men in the Bible who manifestly bear the image of God; Abraham, Isaac, Enoch, Moses, David, John, Paul and others. There have been many men in ancient and modern times who, when some great crisis has come in the state or church, have conducted themselves as men born in the image of God; men who have sacrificed their own interests to be loyal to the truth. We all recognize such men as God-born.

The Evil Man. — The difficulty is however to recognize any image of God in a certain class of evil men who have low instincts and desires; men who lie, cheat, steal and break every commandment of God and man.

Did God make the worst and the lowest of men? If we are to consider fairly the question of the making of man in the image of God we must not shun this problem, which the vilest of men and the most degraded savage presents. What can be seen in these men that reminds us of "the likeness of God"? We are to judge men, however, by what they are capable of and are, at their best, rather than at their worst. The art world regards Michael Angelo's statue of Moses as one of the greatest creations of the sculptor's genius. Suppose, however, some one should maliciously deluge this masterpiece with ink, smash it into fragments with a huge hammer, and then ask as he looked upon the marred and blackened bits of marble, "Is that a masterpiece of Michael Angelo's genius?" So we look upon a man who has been marred and broken by sin and ask the question, "Was that man created in the image of God? Lo, this only have I found, that God hath made man upright; but they have sought out many inventions." Trace back the cause of the degradation of the individual or society or state and we always find the root to be in some transgression of a righteous law of God.

The Bible uniformly asserts that God is not the author of sin or man's fall into evil ways, but that he has sufficient light to follow right ways, if he will. But that an evil man has this marvelous heritage of being God-born is shown by the fact that even when he has marred "the likeness of God" in him, by sin, beyond human recognition there is still a possibility of its being restored. Jesus Christ said, "For the Son of man is come to seek and save that which was lost" (Luke 19:10; Matthew 15:24; Luke 15:4); the most evil men came to Him and, confessing their sins, were brought back into sonship with God. The incentive to Christian work, in the slums of the cities, amongst the most degraded savages and everywhere, is the finding of men broken and marred by sin and the possibility of bringing them back to God.

God disapproves the sin but loves the sinner. "God commended His love towards us in that while we were yet sinners Christ died for us" (Romans 5:8-11).

THE CHIEF END OF MAN

The Bible declares the divine origin and the divine destiny of man, and that he was made in the image of God and for His glory.

A Threefold Obligation rests upon man to serve and glorify God,

"1. On account of his creation by God, the Father.

"2. On account of his redemption by God, the Son.

"3. On account of his regeneration and sanctification by God, the Holy Ghost."

The Great Concern of Man should be conformity with the divine likeness (John 5:30; Matthew 6:10,33; 16:26; Romans 14:8; I Corinthians 10:31). "Be not conformed to this world: but be ye transformed by the renewing of your mind, that ye may prove what is that good and acceptable and perfect will of God" (Romans 12:2). It is only when man succeeds in bringing his will to do God's will and makes God's plan his plan of life that he comes to his best and highest estate. The world is full of sin and misery, and there are many burdens heavy to be borne, because man insists upon having his way instead of seeking God's way. Many great civilizations have gone down and many forms of society have been disrupted because, in them, man strove to set up his glory, rather than God's glory, as the standard to be striven for. Man has repeatedly attempted to attain to "the dominion" promised him only to fail because he has desired such "dominion" to spend it upon himself. God desires to crown man with glory and honour and to do exceedingly large things for him, the Scriptures are filled with great promises, but man only grasps at the shadow of power, when he might have the substance. All great inventions and discoveries but point to still greater ones, when man shall be fitted by spiritual grace and goodness to be intrusted with them. The kingdom of heaven must come in man's heart before any great material or spiritual advancement can come in the world. Education, commerce, art, science, in all their majesty of strength, can never do what the Christian religion can do for men when it shall succeed in getting them to seek to be conformed to "the divine likeness": this is a truth too little emphasized, but it is fundamental and necessary to any real progress in the world. "There is a higher law for life than self-will and unregulated impulse; the real world goes deeper than things of sense; this temporal life is related to eternity; and God is the central verity of all."

THE PERFECT EXAMPLE

God's Measure of a Man. — What is the standard by which man is to compare himself? Great things are expected of a man but how is he to work them out? These are fair questions.

Jesus Christ has two titles in the New Testament, "The Son of God" and "The Son of Man." If we want to know what God is like we look into the face of Jesus Christ. If we want to know what man ought to be we look into the face of Jesus Christ (John 14:5-9; Matthew 5:48).

Jesus Christ is the Perfect Example.

He is the Perfect Example of a Physical Man. — The test here is bodily endurance and perfect control over the body. Look at Jesus Christ and note His physical endurance tests. He was forty days without food (Matthew 4:2); this is not a weakling's task. A man must have a strong body to endure through such a starvation period. For a man to be crucified upon a cross, after being scourged, was to undergo the most terrible agony; yet Christ so had His body under control upon His cross that He could speak forgiveness for His enemies and commend His mother to the care of a disciple. "How can I start a religion?" said one great Frenchman to another. "Go and be crucified," was the reply. If we want to behold the perfect physical man, who had His body in complete control and made it do His will, we must look to Jesus Christ. How many sins come to man through a weak physical control!

He is the Perfect Example of an Intellectual Man. — What man can compare with Jesus Christ in the power of His intellect? He stands ready before all to state and defend His precepts and principles. He so spoke to the people that they listened with growing conviction. "Never man spake like this man." Difficult questions were brought to Him, questions which would make the wisest judges hesitate in their answers, and at once He gave His replies which stand unimpeached to-day for marvellous wisdom and power. Living in an age long before modern science had its birth, He handles Nature as her Master and makes no mistake. His words to-day are a power in the court, in the senate and the marts of the world, as well as in the pulpit. He is the perfect intellectual man for our example.

He is the Perfect Example of a Moral Man. — Many intellectual and physical giants fail upon the moral test; but in Christ we find no moral flaw. He is the standard of moral perfection. He is the perfect moral example for all men.

Here is the foundation for physical and intellectual progress, but without a true moral foundation they will both fail.

No man ever so ministered to men as Jesus Christ.

QUESTIONS

What is man? What shall we think of him? What is the Christian thought of man? Give the five points in the Christian conception of man. Man made in the image of God; give a statement of this case. What is the image of God? Did God make the good man, the evil man? What is the chief end of man? What threefold obligation rests upon man to serve and glorify God? What should be the great concern of man? What can be said of God's measure of a man? What can be said of Jesus Christ as the perfect physical, intellectual and moral man?

STUDY IV

THE CHRISTIAN'S FELLOW MAN

Scripture references: Luke 10:29-37; Matthew 7:12; 5:16; Luke 12:13-15; 1 Corinthians 13; Matthew 7:3-5; 5:42-49; John 21:21, 22.

MAN AND OTHER MEN

The Question of Relationship. — One of the most important questions is that of the relation which a man shall hold to other men.

1. It is fundamental in every system of philosophy and religion. The answers, which are given, show their widespread practical bearing in the social, industrial and political spheres, as well as in the religious.

2. It is imperative from the fact it demands a reply which becomes at once the basis of action. A man, amongst men, is under the necessity of deciding how he will conduct himself towards his fellow men.

There are many divergent opinions, in regard to the relation which a man should sustain to his fellow man, which lead to widely divergent courses of action and largely affect the world for good or ill.

Jesus Christ was outspoken on this matter. His words (Luke 10:29-37; Matthew 22:36-40) go at once to the heart of the question and give its only possible solution.

THE DIFFERENCES BETWEEN MEN

The Inequalities in the Lives of Men are many and far reaching. They divide men from each other and tend, if brooded over, to make them live lives apart, with a lessening sympathy and a growing hostility. They pertain to race, education, business and society. They may be natural, or artificially induced.

The great inequality to-day, however, upon which men place an acute emphasis is that of wealth or the lack of it. A man once came to Jesus and said, "Master, speak to my brother, that he divide the inheritance with me" (Luke 12:13); there is the same demand to-day. Men are not seeking to share the responsibility of a self-denying service to their fellow-men, such as Jesus gave; neither are they greatly desirous of advancing the cause of righteousness in the world, but they are too largely looking to the betterment of their material condition. It is this state of affairs which often spurs men on to accumulate wealth by the oppression of their fellow men. Many men work and plan for certain great results in financial matters (as though these were the supreme things), only to be disappointed and in consequence lose their interest in life. It is the making of the struggle for material betterment the chief thing in life which causes strikes, lockouts and most of our modern industrial troubles. Here we find also the cause of heart-burnings and jealousies and deep-seated hatreds.

It is said that out of these struggles between competitors, and employer and employee, there is coming a better understanding between the contending parties and also new adjustments which will do away with these destructive strifes. This may all be true, but so long as men seek simply and only for material betterment, ignoring the spiritual and moral in their lives, any readjustment of hours of labour or scale of wages or agreements will only be of a temporary character, for the real cause of the whole trouble is left untouched. One of the ablest writers upon "The Social Unrest" says, "At the heart of the larger labour movement is the race longing for a society in which at least the spirit of equality shall be realized. Most radical remedies are only means to this end. Beyond, and deeper than all the machinery of social reconstruction, is this master passion of democracy." But this same writer also, after a survey of the whole question, declares that before this equality can be realized there must come a character founded on love.

Cause and Remedy.—Selfishness is often the real cause of the sting of inequality and of the keeping of men apart; until this is eradicated and replaced by the master passion of love—employer for employee and employee for employer—no agreements and no legislation, between the contending forces will serve the purpose. It was the master passion of a supreme love which produced the first social equality society (Acts 4:32-37); it was selfishness which broke it up (Acts 5:1-13). This selfishness is also at the root of the arrogance which causes men to despise men of an inferior race, culture or social position and seeks to use them for purposes of gain.

Perfect equality amongst men, however, outside of equality before the law and God, hardly seems a realizable thing; certainly all men cannot be of the same age and of the same stature at the same time; there are gifts of talent; there are different races, but where supreme love is it takes out the sting of a sense of an inferiority and the jealousy and hatred of superior gifts; under its benign influence the rich and the poor, the talented and the untalented, work together as brethren. The brotherhood of love is the only true brotherhood and the only solution of this vexed question.

THE TRUE RELATION OF MAN TO MAN

Who is My Neighbour?—The answer which Jesus gave to this question (Luke 10:29), which a certain lawyer asked of Him in order to justify himself, shows the true relation of man to man.

The lawyer doubtless supposed when he put this question to Jesus that he would silence Him. The Jews in their proud isolation considered themselves the chosen people of God and despised other races, even looking with a certain contempt upon their Roman conquerors. How would the Jewish Messiah, if not put to silence, answer a question like this? Doubtless the reply would be that only a Jew could be neighbour to a Jew. The race spirit is a strong one and men born to a certain nationality have many stout binding ties of speech and customs, which are not easily broken.

Mark, however, the large mindedness of Jesus. He breaks at once through race ties and without so much as mentioning the Jew, he takes the Samaritan as the example of a good neighbour. Now the Jews and the Samaritans had no dealings with each other, their animosity was well known; at this distance of time we can hardly realize how startling a thing it was to take a Samaritan as an example of a good neighbour. But it is right here that Jesus begins to show us the true relation of man to man and that this relation is superior to race, caste, language, social distinctions, customs and organizations.

My neighbour, then, is not only the man who lives next door, or is in the same business, or belongs to the same church or labour organization, or political party, but all men are my neighbours and I am to seek to do them good (Luke 10:30-37). This definition of neighbour does away with all clannishness and exclusiveness, and man comes face to face with his fellow man as a man.

How Shall I Treat My Neighbour? — A number of answers may be given:

1. Investigate the claims of my neighbour when I see him in a sad condition. The good Samaritan did this at considerable personal risk, for he could be by no means sure that the robbers would not return and rob him. Too many men, when they see their neighbours in want, pass by on the other side, as the priest and Levite did. Adversity has been described as "a deep pit, into which a man has fallen, which is surrounded by his near-sighted friends."

2. Sympathize and succour my neighbour in trouble and do what is needed to help him get upon his feet.

3. Interest myself in the well being of my neighbour after the immediate and acute necessity for aid is past. There are many who are willing to aid when a pressing call comes, but who are unwilling to keep up that aid through the convalescing stage; here is where the summons comes to be not weary in well doing to one's neighbour.

Outside of money help and aid in times of disaster and sickness there are many who are lonesome for words of cheer and acts of kindness on the part of those with whom they daily come in contact. There is a deeper meaning in the parable than that which relates to physical pain. There is a suffering of the soul and a mental trouble which beseech the kindness of the Christlike neighbourly touch.

4. There is also the larger work, which is fundamental, of bringing one's fellow man into the fellowship and communion of Jesus

Christ; this is the greatest benefit which any Christian man can confer upon his brother-man (John 1:40-42,45).

CHRIST'S LAW OF LOVE

Statement of the Law. — "Thou shalt love thy neighbour as thyself" (Matthew 22:39). A certain lawyer asked Jesus, "Master, which is the great commandment of the law? Jesus said unto him, Thou shalt love the Lord thy God with all thy heart, and with all thy soul and with all thy mind. This is the first and great commandment. And the second is like unto it. Thou shalt love thy neighbour as thyself." The kingdom of God will come when this commandment is fully obeyed by men.

Exposition of the Law. — It would seem as if a law so plainly stated would need no explanation or exposition. But before men can rightly love each other they must have certain principles and a certain character. It is not desirable that evil men with depraved thoughts and bad lives love us as they love themselves; for they love that which, if accepted by men, would lead to deep corruption of character.

Jesus Christ well put it that God must first be loved, with all the heart, soul and mind, before a man is ready to love his neighbour as himself. This loving of God, first, implies an acceptance of the standpoint of God in regard to man and the looking upon one's fellow man as God looks upon him. This standpoint of God is best seen in the words and acts of Jesus Christ. A man in order, then, to love his fellow man aright must be thoroughly imbued with the principles of the Master. A man must look upon other men as having souls of eternal value. A man who would do as Jesus would have him do must first have His spirit of self-sacrificing love (Matthew 23:8-12; John 17:19; Philippians 2:5-7; Isaiah 53:3; John 13:12-15).

Application of the Law. — The beauty of this law of love is that it may be universally applied. There is no condition of man that it cannot meet and satisfy. The crying wrongs of the home, society, the industrial world, the state, arise out of its neglect and condemnation. Men seek to make good their claims for things which they think belong to them, they fight for them, gain them or lose them, fight again or are fought, and in consequence race hatred, class and industrial hatred embitter the hearts of men.

This law applied to the life of the individual, sweetens it in its lowest depths and makes the strongest kind of a character. Paul is an example of an able yet impetuous man, who let the gospel of the love of Christ have its supreme way with him. We find in him no shrinking from difficulties or death itself (2 Timothy 4:6-8). In the midst of sore trials he wrote that remarkable classic (1 Corinthians 13) upon love which has been the help and stay of many a burdened soul.

This law applied in society is its only saving power. It is this Christ love which sends men into the slums of the cities to work for their fellow men. It is this love that is the moving power of the missionary of the cross, when he goes into the heart of heathendom. It is this love that has brought into the world all the reforms that are worth having and caused it to care for its sick and its poor.

It is to be deplored that in some quarters we should hear voices talking about the inability of the Church to cope with the modern conditions of life and that these voices should be calling for new institutions to take its place. So long as the Church recognizes its duty to preach and practice the love of God to man, man to God, and man to his fellow man, no institution can take its place; for it has in this preaching, and the application of it, the supreme remedy for the ills of mankind. Where there is no love or regard of man for his God or fellow men all agreements and all laws however stoutly made, with and for contending parties, have in them a fatal weakness.

It is love that sent Jesus Christ into the world (John 3:16,17) and it is its proclamation, and acceptance as the ruling power of life, that has caused all the real advancement in civilization since His advent.

QUESTIONS

What can be said of the question of the relationship of man to other men? What can be said of the inequalities in the lives of men and the great inequality? What is the cause and remedy of the sting of inequality? Who is my neighbour? How shall I treat my neighbour? What is Christ's law of love? Give the statement, exposition and application of the law.

STUDY V

THE CHRISTIAN FAITH

Scripture references: Hebrews 11; Matthew 9:29; 17:20; Mark 10:52; 11:22; Acts 2:38; 3:16; 10:43; 16:30,31; Romans 1:17; 5:1; 10:17; Galatians 2:20.

FAITH AND PRACTICE

Belief Controls Action. — "As the man is, so is his strength" (Judges 8:21), "For as he thinketh in his heart so is he" (Proverbs 23:7). "According to your faith be it unto you" (Matthew 9:28,29). "Keep thy heart with all diligence; for out of it are the issues of life" (Proverbs 4:23).

The Scriptures place stress upon the fact that a man's actions are largely dependent upon what he believes or disbelieves rather than upon his environment (Proverbs 4:23; Romans 10:10; Acts 8:21; Matthew 9:4; 12:34; 15:11,18-20; 23:25).

There is the will to believe and there is the will not to believe (Matthew 15:28; 16:24; Luke 9:23; John 5:40). Man grows from the inside out. What he believes in his heart will sooner or later manifest itself in his acts. If a man thinks evil in his heart and cherishes that evil, while outwardly his life is moral and upright, it is only a question of time when the inner badness will break through the thin crust of outer goodness. The real battle of life is in a man's soul and if a man sets himself to win this battle he need have no fear of outward evil circumstances; he will have to set no guard upon his words or acts for he will speak and act from a pure and upright heart. It is not what he disbelieves, but what he believes, his conviction of truth, that makes him strong.

Hence the necessity for the vigorous and living faith which Christ urged upon His followers (Mark 11:22-24; Matthew 17:19,20; Luke 8:

24,25), a faith that could not be daunted by mountains of difficulty or great storms of afflictions.

Jesus came into the world with a positive program. He had a constructive gospel to preach to men. His disciples after His death followed in the footsteps of their Master and carried out His commands. The result was that faith was translated into action; the old world was changed and myriads of men gave in their allegiance to the Christ. The positive setting forth of the Christian faith always brings definite results.

BASIS OF CHRISTIAN FAITH

The Christian Faith is Founded Upon the Fact and Experience of Jesus
Christ. — Without Him there would have been no such faith.

1. The fact of Christ. This faith bases itself primarily not upon reason or feeling, but upon Jesus Christ, a historical person, and what He said and did while upon this earth in bodily form. The early disciples and preachers declared themselves to be witnesses. They were sent forth as witnesses (Matthew 28:18-20; John 15:27; Acts 1:8; 2: 32). The speeches of Peter (Acts 2:14-40; 3:12-26; 4:8-12), Stephen (Acts 7:1-56) and of Paul (Acts 13:16-41; 22:1-21) are recitals, of certain well attested occurrences, which have for their chief point the setting forth of the fact of Jesus Christ, the Son of God, as the Saviour of men and hope of the world (Acts 2:38,39).

2. The experience of Christ. By this is meant the experience which men have who receive Christ as their Saviour and Lord. There is a historical Christ; and there is a spiritual Christ who enters into a communion of happiness and joy, with believers in Him. Jesus Christ, when on earth in bodily form, promised the coming of the Holy Spirit who should glorify Him (John 16:13,14); He also declared to His disciples, "Lo, I am with you alway, even unto the end of the world" (Matthew 28:20). Wherever this gospel of Jesus Christ is preached and men under its power truly repent of their sins and accept Him as their Saviour, as in the past so now, men may enter into personal relations with their risen and glorified Lord (Acts 2:40-

42; John 7:17; Acts 8: 5-7; Romans 8:1-10; Colossians 1:27; Acts 26:15-19).

Essential Elements. — In the Christian faith there are six component elements.

1. Belief in God as The Spirit, "infinite, eternal, and unchangeable in His being, wisdom and power, holiness, justice, goodness and truth" (John 4:24; Exodus 20:2-7; Deuteronomy 6:4; Isaiah 44:6; John 17:3; 1 Corinthians 8:4,6; Psalm 19; 104:24).

2. Belief in man, as a child of God, whose spirit is destined to live forever (Genesis 2:7; 2 Corinthians 5:1; Ecclesiastes 12:7; Matthew 6:25; 5:29,30).

3. Belief in sin which taints and corrupts the heart of man, making it finally, if unchecked, the dwelling place of all evil. The effects of sin are everywhere plainly manifest. Men not only sin through ignorance and carelessly but willfully. The worst sins are those which are of the spirit, anger, pride, malice and envy (Isaiah 53:6; 64:6; Romans 3:23; 1 John 1:8; Romans 1:18-3:23; 8:7).

4. Belief in Jesus Christ, the Son of God and the Saviour of men, who can cleanse the heart of man and save him from his sins. Jesus Christ came not only to reveal God, the Father, to man but also to purge his heart from evil. "He is the propitiation for our sins" (1 John 2:1,2; Romans 8:34; Hebrews 7:24,25; Matthew 20:28; Romans 3:24,25; 5:8; 8:3; Galatians 3:13; 2 Corinthians 5:21; 1 Corinthians 1:30; Matthew 9:2-6).

5. Belief in the sanctifying power of the Holy Spirit (1 Corinthians 6:11; Ephesians 3:16; Galatians 5:22) who "testifies of Christ, as the Saviour of sinners, unites us to Him by faith, and makes us partakers of all His benefits." Jesus said, "When the Comforter is come, whom I will send unto you from the Father, even the Spirit of truth, which proceedeth from the Father, He shall testify of Me" (John 15:26). "The Spirit of truth ... will guide you into all truth.... He shall glorify Me: for He shall receive of Mine and shall show it unto you" (John 16:13,14; 14:26; 1 Corinthians 12:3; Titus 3:5,6; Matthew 28: 19; John 3:5,6).

6. Belief in the resurrection and the life to come, the issues of which are declared to be eternal. "The hour is coming in which all

that are in the graves shall hear His voice, and shall come forth; they that have done good, unto the resurrection of life; and they that have done evil, unto the resurrection of damnation" (John 5:28,29; Matthew 25:31-46; 25:1-13). The great rainbow of promise that spans the future, for those who trust in Christ, is in the fact that He said, "I am the resurrection and the life: he that believeth in Me, though he were dead, yet shall he live. And whosoever liveth and believeth in Me shall never die" (John 11:25,26; I Thessalonians 5:23; John 6:47; 14:2,19). The resurrection body "will be spiritual, immortal, incorruptible, and like unto the glorious body of Jesus Christ" (Philippians 3:20,21; 1 Corinthians 15:20-23,35-57).

Definiteness.—There is a marvellous directness and definiteness in the statements of the New Testament writers, in proclaiming the Christian faith, because they believe that they are dealing with the tremendous facts of life and destiny. God has manifested Himself and spoken in Jesus Christ as He has never manifested Himself before. "God who at sundry times and in diverse manners spake in time past unto the fathers by the prophets, hath in these last days spoken unto us by His Son, whom He hath appointed heir of all things" (Hebrews 1:1,2). The eternal things of God, kept secret from the foundation of the world, are now made known to man; why should he not, in spite of any punishment or threatened ignominious death, proclaim these truths definitely and plainly to his fellow man (Acts 4:13-20)?

The keynote of all of Paul's work is sounded in a very definite and direct way in his first Epistle to the Corinthians (2:2,5) where he says, "For I determined not to know anything among you, save Jesus Christ and Him crucified.... That your faith should not stand in the wisdom of men but in the power of God." Paul consistently maintains throughout his Epistles that the sole basis of salvation is the grace of God through Jesus Christ, to be appropriated by faith on the part of man.

TESTS OF CHRISTIAN FAITH

Effects Upon Men and Institutions.—Jesus Christ was ever urging His disciples to test His words and principles. He declared the difference between true and false prophets could be known by their fruits. He said, "Do men gather grapes of thorns or figs of thistles? Even so every good tree bringeth forth good fruit; but a corrupt tree bringeth forth evil fruit … wherefore by their fruits ye shall know them" (Matthew 7:15-20). When Thomas expressed doubt of His resurrection, Christ gave him ample opportunity to test its reality (John 20:24-29). Christ's challenge to the world is, "Try Me!" "Come and see what I can do!"

What kind of men has the Christian faith made? What kind of communities has it produced? Two pertinent questions are asked in a recent book of sermons, What would be the effect upon this world if everybody was a consistent Christian? What would be the effect upon this world if everybody was a consistent infidel? "The argument is a crushing one, for of a truth Christianity can stand such a test with a glory that would astonish even the most ardent enthusiasts. And it is the one test, let it be admitted with sorrow, that a reviling world is not willing to have it judged by."

A Saving Faith which meets men at their extremity of need and gives them a new heart. It is not only a faith that did save men when Christ walked the earth and healed the sick, giving sight to the blind and raising the dead, but it is a faith which saves men now. Christ is still performing His miracle of cleansing the hearts of men of evil. He is saying, "Come unto Me," and men are coming as of old. The question whether He can save now is being put to the test every day and every day it is being answered in the regeneration of men. Wherever this gospel is preached amongst the wealthy and learned or the poor and ignorant, it shows its splendid fruitage as it did of old.

USES OF CHRISTIAN FAITH

To Make Plain the Great Cause of All as Father. — We live in an immense universe, in the midst of giant forces of which, after science has made its most searching investigation and said its last word, we know comparatively little and that little imperfectly. No set of men is more ready to admit this state of affairs than that which has made the closest scrutiny of the phenomena of nature.

There is a host of questions to which the most painstaking investigation on the part of the philosophers can afford us no answer.

Without this Christian faith which tells us of a revelation from God and His plan and purpose for man we should be helpless, ever seeking for light in this universe which we could not find. Then again we might believe in a first great cause of all things, but without a revelation we could not know God as the Creator of all things and as our Father who cares supremely for us—made known in the manifestation of Jesus Christ.

By faith in Christ we are brought into communion with God the Father.

To Show the Importance and Value of Human Life.—How could man know that he was more than an atom in a whirlpool of atoms, his life of sense but a transitory thing, if it had not been for the Scriptures which seek to impress upon him the value of his life in the sight of God (John 3:16,17; Matthew 16:26)? Without the pale of the Christian faith men hold life but cheaply, they squander it and waste it in sin; they too often say, "Let us eat, drink and be merry for tomorrow we die"—forever passing out of existence. The Christian faith holds human life as a very precious thing, something to be cherished with infinite and loving care, for the spirit in man is to live forever. Here is a new significance given to life which, when the individual accepts it, gives him new and great ideals, which lift him to a higher level of living.

By faith in Christ we are brought into proper fellowship with our fellow men, and their lives are made precious in our sight.

To Show the Way to Happiness and Joy Through Jesus Christ.—If there is one thing more than another which man is seeking it is happiness, but it is the kind of happiness which frequently destroys the body and soul—still he seeks it. Many men seek happiness through relaxation of their moral nature.

Christ came preaching the happiness of a conqueror, the victor who sings the song of rejoicing over some victory won; He set forth a joy which celebrated a conquest over evil desires and made a man noble and pure in his thoughts and aspirations. Jesus did His work for the joy that was set before Him (Hebrews 12:2). The Christian faith was never intended to make a man gloomy or downcast, but to put joy in his heart and a song upon his lips. No one has more right to a cheerful countenance than the sincere Christian, for he can be sure that he knows the way of happiness here and nothing can come to him hereafter save peace and glory in the redeemed life.

QUESTIONS

How does belief control action? What is the basis of Christian faith? Give the six component elements of the Christian faith. What can be said of the definiteness of the Christian faith? Give some of the tests of Christian faith. Give three uses of Christian faith.

STUDY VI

THE CHRISTIAN'S BOOK

Scripture references 2 Timothy 3:16,17; 2 Peter 1:20,21; John 5:39; Romans 15:4; 2 Samuel 23:2; Luke 1:70; 24:32,45; John 2:22; 10:35; 19:36; Acts 1:16; Romans 1:1,2; 1 Corinthians 15:3,4; James 2:8.

WHAT IS THE BIBLE?

What is the Bible? How shall we regard it? Where shall we place it? These and many questions like them at once come to the front when we begin to discuss the Bible as a book. It is only possible in this brief study, of a great subject, to indicate the line of some of the answers.

It is not Like Other Books. — Although its last paragraph was written and the canon completed many hundreds of years ago, it is still one of the freshest and newest of books and its moral precepts and admonitions are far in advance of the world's practice. It has an adaptability to all sorts and conditions of men and a flexibility in meeting the most radical changes of thought, which is possessed by no other volume. It has been attacked and denounced and seemingly demolished only in the end to lead its critics captive and to come forth from the fray stronger than ever.

It is a God-filled and God-inspired book. It is the most lasting in its popularity of all books.

It is Like Other Books in that it is cast in the mold of the literature of a certain people. We find here all the forms of literature, history, philosophy, poetry, letters, etc. There is much plausibility in the plea for the study of the Bible as literature for it is the best of its kind.

It Leads the World's Thought of Righteousness and Purity of Life. — The

Ten Commandments (Exodus 20:1-17), The Beatitudes (Matthew 5:1-12) and
The Sermon on the Mount (Matthew 5:1-7:29) set forth the highest ethical standards known to man.

It is the Record of a Revelation from God.

The theme is, "the entrance of God into the spiritual life of man." This makes it superior to all other books and invests it with a unique character which commands our most earnest attention. God, who is speaking to men through this book, says, "Thou shalt have no other gods before Me." God is not only the God of the Israelites but of all nations and peoples.

The great men, whose life stories are given in the Bible, were God called to, and God guided in, their work of uplifting the world. We have only to look at the record to see how the initiative is declared to have been taken by God. Here is the roll call, Abraham (Genesis 12:1-3), Moses (Exodus 3:14), Joshua (1:1-6), Samuel (1 Samuel 3:4-21), David (1 Samuel 16:3,11-13), Isaiah (1:1), Ezekiel (1:1), Jeremiah (1:2) and all the prophets, John the Baptist (Luke 1:13-17; Matthew 3:1-12), Peter, John and Paul (Acts 1:8; 2:1-4; 13:1,2).

The Old Testament shows the looking forward to the Christ and the New Testament records His coming as the Spiritual Light of the world. No other book or set of books announce "the entrance of God to the spiritual life of man" through Jesus Christ (John 1:1-18), who came speaking of the new spiritual birth of man (John 3:1-21).

The only key to the understanding of the Bible is this plan of God to enter into the spiritual life of man. We may easily look in the Bible for what is not there and read into its pages what is in our own thoughts or read out of them that which we do not wish to see, but back of all we must acknowledge this peculiar purpose of God.

Back also of all theories of revelation and inspiration—and giving rise to them—stands the great thought of God for the spiritual redemption of men. For this end He enters into covenant with the Israelites, He sends them prophets and teachers, and at last He sends His Son. Continually God is calling to men, "Be ye holy for I am holy."

STRUCTURE

In any book, after the consideration of the theme, we look for the form and the plan. In order to study a book to the best advantage, the different parts and their relation to each other and to the whole must be made plain. The Bible readily lends itself to an investigation of its structure.

The Bible is One Book with one thought running through it, God's purpose to redeem man, and may be so read and studied.

The Bible is Composed of Many Books written by different authors in different languages, at different times. Some of the books were circulated separately before they were gathered either into the canon of the Old or New Testaments. The gathering together of the books and the placing them in the order that we have them now was a slow process, but all in the order and interest of a progressive revelation of God and because of a common sympathetic subject.

The books take different forms and have different classifications, such as books of the law, wisdom, history, poetry, etc. In studying any book it is necessary to attend to its classification; there has been much misunderstanding of the Bible books because of the interpretation of a book of poetry as history or the holding the free style of a letter to the hard and fast standards of a carefully worded court document. The standpoint of the author of a book, and some consideration for the age in which he lives, must always be taken into consideration; in this way a book, which may seem to us now to be behind the age in its thought, will be seen to be far ahead of the age in which the author lived and making and marking an important epoch in a progressive revelation.

Each Bible book has a well considered plan, a special aim, a historical setting and a practical value. For instance, in Genesis we have a book of beginnings; a broad explanation of the origin of the world, man, sin, salvation; and the revelation of God as Creator, Preserver, Lawgiver, Judge and Merciful Father. After the introduction the book, if we look into the book itself, is divided into ten parts with the recurring formula, "These are the generations of." This book cannot be overestimated from a religious standpoint. The fact of a Creator is the fundamental teaching of its cosmogony. God, one God, is here clearly distinguished from a host of heathen gods. He is over and above matter, everything in the universe is subject to Him. Again in this book we have the early history of the human race shown in large outline and also the story of the fathers of the Jewish race from the calling of Abraham to the death of Jacob. Behind any theory of the construction of Genesis the great representative truths stand firm. Every Bible book can be considered and its plan and purpose shown in this way. Even a small book like Ruth, which seems to be only a little pleasant story, has an important part to perform. Without it the times of the judges would present only a very somber picture, but with it we can see that in those dark and troublous times there were noble, God fearing men like Boaz and true women like Ruth. We could not spare a single book of the New Testament, for with one lacking something would be wanting in the picture of early Christianity.

The Bible is Composed of Groups of Books Which Relate to Special Eras. — They show God revealing Himself and also dealing with the chosen nation, under different forms of administration; they indicate the steps leading up to Christ and His appearance on the earth.

First Era, the Time of Beginnings (Genesis 1-11:32). This extends from the creation of the world to the call of Abraham. We have here set forth the connection of the world with God, the beginning of life and beginning of sin, which rendered salvation necessary.

Second Era, the Theocracy. The record is found in the books of Genesis, Exodus, Leviticus, Numbers, Deuteronomy, Joshua, Judges, Ruth and 1 Samuel. This period is known as the Theocracy because it marks the direct rule of God over His people. It lasted from the covenant of God with Abraham to the anointing of Saul as king. We here see the beginning of the chosen family, and nation, what laws and precepts were given it and what fortunes befell it. This training time shows God's high standards in the laws and precept given this Israelitish people.

Third Era, the Monarchy. The record is found in the books of 1 and 2 Samuel, 1 and 2 Kings, 1 and 2 Chronicles, Psalms, Jonah, Amos, Hosea, Micah, Joel, Isaiah, Nahum, Zephaniah, Habakkuk and Jeremiah. We have here the story of the rise, glory, division and fall of the Jewish monarchy. The people desired a king and the king sought to rule by his own will rather than the will of God. We note God's desire to make this nation a "Holy Nation" and its sin and failure. The function of the prophets was to declare the sin of the nation, to set the right way before it and seek to lead it back to God, but the nation would not heed the voices of the prophets, hence the fall of the monarchy. The coming of the perfect king and kingdom under the Messiah is prophesied. The work and place of Christ is foretold by the prophets.

Fourth Era, the Captivity. The record is found in the books of 2 Chronicles, Jeremiah, Daniel, Ezekiel and Obadiah. The people rejecting God are taken into captivity. In this captivity the people turn to God in their affliction, their worship is purified and the hope of the coming of the Messiah grows very strong.

Fifth Era, the Restoration. The record is found in the books of Ezra, Nehemiah, Haggai, Zechariah and Malachi. The people purified by their captivity and uplifted by their hope of the coming Christ are restored to their own land.

Sixth Era, the Christian. The record is found in the books of the New Testament. The Christian era is ushered in by the coming of Christ and the fulfillment of God's promises. The mission of the Jewish nation finds its fruition in Christ and the coming of the Saviour of all mankind.

It will be seen from this very brief summary of the eras how God gradually revealed Himself and His plan for the spiritual enlightenment of all men. The necessity also of studying each book, not only in its own plan but in its group place, in order to find its meaning, cannot be too earnestly commended.

CREDIBILITY

It is natural that a book demanding our belief in such great things should be asked for its credentials and that these credentials should be subjected to the most searching investigation. The Bible has nothing to fear, however, from the keenest scrutiny of any scholar who has only the desire to get at the truth. The trouble begins when a critic, who is hostile to its spiritual truth or who has a theory to maintain, takes a part in the investigation; even then the truth is sure, in time, to assert its rightful claim (Acts 5:39). The fact of different interpretations of the same set of facts in different times, but leading to the same practical results, must also be taken into consideration. All men do not receive the same truth in the same way while they may be one at heart in the fundamentals (1 Corinthians 12:4-14).

The Bible welcomes any and all searching of its claims; it stands out in the open; it has won its way amongst mankind not by the might of those who advocate its claims, but by the power of the truth within its pages.

Some of the arguments for the credibility of the Bible are here given.

The Argument from History.—Back of all questions of authorship, date and composition of the books of the Bible, is the one great question, Are the records true to the facts? Is the Bible, in plain words, true history?

The writers of the New Testament use the historical argument. They speak of the things most surely believed amongst us and of the testimony of eyewitnesses (Luke 1:1-4; John 19:35; 21:24,25). The disciples were not to go forth preaching a subtle philosophy, but were to be witnesses of certain facts and were to testify of the things which they had seen and heard (Acts 1:8). Peter's speech upon the day of Pentecost is a recital of facts. Paul's argument for the resurrection of Christ is based upon the testimony of eye-witnesses (1 Corinthians 15:1-20). If God has manifested Himself in the person of Jesus Christ we need to know it through the best of testimony in regard to the fact. The record of the New Testament is made to this end.

The writers of the Old Testament profess to give us statements of facts in regard to God's dealings with the Israelitish people. The critical dealing with each of the books of the Old Testament is all to the intent whether it fairly represents a historical situation. The older scriptural narratives show of the doings of other nations than the Israelites, they describe situations in times long past, where owing to broken and imperfect records, it has been difficult to get at the exact facts. Unfortunately in some quarters the tendency has been to cast doubt upon the Old Testament writings where the statements were not corroborated by a research in the archives, often very imperfect, of other nations. But happily this state of affairs is being changed and confidence in the historicity of the Old Testament records is being greatly strengthened by the investigations of the archaeologists in the ruins of the great empires of Egypt, Assyria and Babylonia with which Israel came so closely in contact. Until recently the Old Testament stood alone in its assertion of a comparatively high civilization antedating Moses and Abraham, but now we know from excavations made in Nippur and other buried cities that the contention of the Bible is true to the letter. The situation in Egypt and Palestine about the time of the Exodus is made plain by the Tel-el-Amarna tablets. The history of first and second Kings is not only corroborated but amplified by the monuments. Much yet remains to be done along this line, some views may have to be changed, but the period of destruction has passed and that of construction has begun.

The Argument from Prophecy.—The Old Testament prophets were not only the preachers of righteousness for their own times and their own nation, but they had a mission to other nations and times as well. Their ruling idea was the establishment of God's kingdom upon earth. They taught the unity, spirituality, holiness, justice and goodness of God. They made predictions in regard to Egypt, Babylon, Assyria, Syria, Moab, and their cities, when they were at the height of their power; these predictions were remarkably fulfilled. They foretold the captivity and restoration of Israel. Their great subject was the expectation of the Messiah and the Messianic Kingdom. The prophecies in regard to the Christ became more and more explicit as the time drew near; they declared His mission, His prophetic power, His kingly office, His priestly activity, the circumstances of His coming through a man, a nation, and in a definite place.

The Arguments from Vitality, Adaptability and Growth.

1. Vitality. The religions of Babylon, Egypt, Greece and Rome died with the nations which gave birth to them. The religion of the Bible, shows its divine author in its vitality and power to outlast the religions with which it has come in contact. Empires, systems of

thought, mighty kings, great men rise and have their day and pass away, but this book lives on. Here is a vitality which persists in spite of any and all adverse circumstances and influences.

2. Adaptability. The Bible is at home with all races in all climes. It adapts itself to all conditions of life, the most humble and the most exalted. The Asiatic, the African, the European, the American accept it as their book. It finds men, as men, in the deepest needs of their nature and shows them the all loving Saviour.

3. Growth. The multiplying power of the book is shown by its translations into hundreds of languages and dialects. It makes its own way into the remotest quarters of the globe and is found wielding its power in the hut and the palace. More popular than any book that has ever been published, its sales, of millions of copies a year are ever increasing, because it comes with a message from God direct to the heart of man.

QUESTIONS

What is the Bible? How is it not like and how is it like other books? How is it the record of a revelation from God? What can be said of its structure? What can be said of its books, of its groups of books? What can be said of its credibility? Give the arguments from history, prophecy, vitality, adaptability and growth.

STUDY VII

THE CHRISTIAN PRAYER

Scripture references: Matthew 6:5-15; Luke 11:1-13; John 17; Matthew
26:41; Mark 11:24,25; Luke 6:12,28; 9:29; 1 Thessalonians 5:17,25; 1
Corinthians 14:13,15; Psalm 19:14; 50:15, Matthew 7:7; 1 Timothy 2:1;
Ephesians 3:20,21; John 16:23; 14:14; James 5:16.

THE PROVINCE OF PRAYER

Definition. — Prayer is the communion of man with God. It is not
first of all the means of getting something from God, but the realization of Him in the soul. "Seek ye first the Kingdom of God and His
righteousness" (Matthew 6:33). The glory of a man is in his upright-
ness of character, the purity of his spirit and his nearness and likeness to God. Man becomes like that which he thinks about the most
often and with which he most frequently communes in the secret
recesses of his heart. Prayer is not merely, then, a matter of stated
times and seasons, although these should be observed, but a constant walking with God and a realization of His presence at all times
and in all places (Luke 18:1; Romans 12:12; 1 Thessalonians 5:17).
The man who thus communes with God will lay before Him his
plans and purposes and will ask for direction and guidance in them;
he will expect help from God as a partner in all his enterprises; he
will grasp the power unseen to work great things in the seen. There
will be special needs and occasions when a man, in harmony with
God (James 5:16), will require special help and for this aid from God
he will make strong and earnest petitions to Him. "Call upon Me in
the day of trouble: I will deliver thee and thou shalt glorify Me"
(Psalm 50:15; James 1:17; Psalm 19:14; Ephesians 3:20,21).

The Different Kinds of Prayer.—They are adoration, thanksgiving, intercession, petition and praise (1 Timothy 2:1).

The Different Places of Prayer.—1. In the public assemblage (Psalm 122:1,2; Acts 3:1; Hebrews 10:25). 2. In the social and family gathering (Matthew 18:19,20; Acts 1:14; 2:46; 12:12). 3. In private (Matthew 6:6; Mark 1:35; Psalm 55:17; Daniel 6:10).

The Approach of Man to God.—"All men pray at some time or other, whether fitfully or constantly, in weakness or in strength, in sorrow or in joy. Some men pray because it is their chiefest delight to do so, and some pray because necessity drives them to it; but they all pray. Prayer is a constant element, and the impulse to pray is ever present to human nature." Man has been called "a religious and praying animal," because of this universal desire of men to come into some touch with the power over them. This tendency is shown in lands where the true spiritual knowledge of God is lacking and where men deify and adore objects of nature. The sun, the earth, the stars, trees, mountains, waters, winds and carved images have all been made divine objects of adoration and prayer, because of the desire of man to find or place the supernatural in them. Paul said to the men of Athens when he saw the altar to the "Unknown God": "Whom therefore ye ignorantly worship Him declare I unto you" (Acts 17:23). All the research of natural science is to find out what is the Ultimate Power behind all the phenomena of nature. Man by his very nature seeks to approach God. He is driven by an inward impulse to come to Him. Hence, where men do not have the true light by which to approach God or reject it there are found all sorts and kinds of caricatures of religion.

What are the proper means of approach to God through prayer?

1. Right knowledge and faith. "He that cometh to God must believe that He is, and that He is a rewarder of them that diligently seek Him" (Hebrews 11:6). "This is life eternal that they might know Thee the only true God and Jesus Christ whom Thou hast sent" (John 17:3). God is above all and in all. There are no other gods before Him. He is supreme, manifested as Father, Son and Holy Spirit. We come at once here to the Great Personal Power, beyond whom there is no greater. We do not look upon Him as a cold abstraction or blind force, but as a loving, kind Father. He desires to do more

for us than we can ask or think. No man prays to God in the right way who does not first of all have a proper conception of God.

2. Right attitude of the heart. "If I regard iniquity in my heart the Lord will not hear me" (Psalm 66:18). Again the prayerless prayer of the Pharisee began with "I" and the burning of incense before himself. No man, cherishing something in his heart which he knows to be contrary to the will of God or who only seeks to foster and advance his own selfish interests, will come, or desire to come, or can come into a very close communion with God. A wrong attitude of the heart keeps many men from the enjoyment of God's presence, and makes them choose to remain away from His sanctuary. No matter what the sin, however, if a man truly desires to get it out of his heart that man can come at once into close touch with God (Isaiah 1:15-19; Psalm 51; Revelation 7:14).

3. Right subjects of prayer. The advancement of the Kingdom of God and the spiritual interests of man come first. Too many prayers move in the narrow circles of self and purely physical wants; they take no wide sweep out over larger interests. God knows that we have physical needs that must be supplied (Matthew 6:26). Jesus said, "Is not the life more than meat and the body than raiment" (Matthew 6:25)? And by His urgency He would have our prayers rise higher than our physical wants into an infinitely larger sphere. Then God will more than bless us and take care of those things about which we are now so anxious (Matthew 6:26-34).

4. Persistency (Matthew 11:12). It is difficult to deny a persistent man who, when thwarted in one way, begins to plan and act for the object which he seeks in another way and who will not be put off. Christ commended the way of the persistent man to those who sought God in prayer. He gave examples of the widow who continually importuned an unjust judge until he listened to her plea and gave her justice (Luke 18:1-8), and of the man who would not take "no" for an answer when he wanted to borrow bread from a neighbour at midnight (Luke 11:5-8). He said, "Ask, and it shall be given unto you; seek, and ye shall find; knock, and it shall be opened unto you" (Luke 11:9). Men who do not persist in their praying will fail to receive the higher blessings and the larger benefits which otherwise God would gladly bestow upon them. If men know how to give

good gifts to their children when they ask for them, then much more God knows how to grant the best things to men when they ask Him. "The kingdom of heaven suffereth violence, and the violent take it by force" (Matthew 11:12).

The Approach of God to Man.—How does God come near to man? Does He hear when men pray to Him? Can He and will He answer prayer?

These questions are all simply and plainly answered in the Scriptures. There is no doubt expressed here that God comes near to men and will hear and answer when they pray to Him. "The Lord is nigh unto all them that call upon Him, to all that call upon Him in truth" (Psalm 145:18; 139:7-12; Ephesians 3:20).

Christian experience answers these questions in the same affirmative way. Multitudes of Christians testify that God comes near to them and that He hears and answers their prayers; there are many recorded and remarkable answers to prayers.

It is only when the testimony of the Bible and the experience of Christians are set aside that difficulties appear which seem very formidable.

One of the chief objections urged against God hearing and answering prayer is the discovery of the widening sphere of what is called natural law in the ordering of the universe. Where God was formally looked upon as directly controlling in certain things, it is pointed out that we now can plainly state the causes and the working of the laws which produce certain results. According to one theory God is shut out of His universe; and according to another, He is shut up in His universe; on either hypothesis the direct control is out of His hands. Hence, "why pray?" when our prayers even if they reach God cannot be answered.

This objection from the domination of law annuls the freedom of God. It is like looking at a great piece of complicated machinery, and having it explained how part depends upon part and, because the dependence is plainly shown, being asked to believe that the maker and controller is under its power. We are asked to-day to concentrate our attention upon the levers, the springs and the pulleys and all the machinery of the universe rather than upon the first great Cause and Ruler of all.

It is assumed in this objection that much more is known of the laws and forces which govern the universe than really is. Prof. John Fiske says in his lecture on "Life Everlasting," I once heard Herbert Spencer say, "you cannot take up any problem in physics without being quickly led to some metaphysical problem which you can neither solve nor evade." Again he says, "The more things we try to explain, the better we realize that we live in a world of unexplained residua."

Widening knowledge is throwing back into the lumber room many much vaunted theories of origins. Many wrong conceptions of the order of nature have in recent years been radically changed. It is freely acknowledged to-day by the foremost men of science that no man fully understands the order of nature. Under the present limitations of human knowledge God cannot be shut up in or out of His universe. Further research may show that such shutting up to be impossible; for in the end we are to depend not upon our ignorance but upon our knowledge of the universe for God's free control of all things.

Already the light begins to dawn when it is seen that all the natural forces and matter itself are beginning to reveal their origin and control in one Great Master Force. But in this we but return to the biblical statement "In the beginning God" (Genesis 1:1).

We are perfectly justified in believing, in the intelligence of God when we see so many evidences of intelligence in the world, and the freedom and personality of God, when we note the freedom and personality of man; for however we may argue that man is not free or personal we believe that he is and act upon this belief in all the practical affairs of life. The created thing is not greater than its creator or the law greater than the lawgiver. God is greater than the universe or man. God as all powerful, and as intelligent and personal can be approached by man and comes near to him through his communion in prayer with Him.

It is perfectly possible for God, in His providential wisdom and power, to answer the prayers of His people. It is an every-day occurrence for man to deflect the beams of the sun and make nature's laws do what they would not have done if left to themselves. We know men to be personal and to be changed by petitions to their mercy and entreaties to use their power in certain directions. We believe that God, infinitely greater than man, can be entreated and will use His power for the benefit of the petitioner. It is not unreasonable for men to pray for material and spiritual blessings. While the sphere of prayer may be narrowed in certain directions by what we know of nature's processes, it has been greatly widened in other directions.

THE MODEL PRAYER

This is the Lord's Prayer which Christ gave His disciples when He preached the Sermon on the Mount (Matthew 6:9-13) and when one of His disciples said to Him, "Lord teach us to pray" (Luke 11:2-4). "It is the prayer of prayers. It is the best and most beautiful, the simplest and yet the deepest, the shortest and yet the most comprehensive of all forms of devotion. Only from the lips of the Son of God could such a perfect pattern proceed. It embraces all kinds of prayer—petition, intercession and thanksgiving; all essential objects of prayer, spiritual and temporal, divine and human, in the most suitable and beautiful order."

It has been divided, and this is the natural division, into three parts, an address, six petitions and a doxology.

The Address.—"Our Father who art in heaven" (Matthew 6:9). This phrase "Our Father" shows the paternal relation which the Almighty sustains to us in Christ and the filial relation which we bear to Him through faith in Christ. It also reminds us that since we have a common Father in God, we are all brothers in Christ. The phrase, "Who art in heaven" shows us our heavenly origin and that our home is in our Father's house. We use the word "our" before Father and by it mean to embrace in prayer all the children of God. In using the word, "Father" we at once say we believe in a personal good God at the heart of all things and controlling all, one who loves and cares for us supremely (Galatians 3:26; Ephesians 2:19; Psalm 103:13; Matthew 7:11; John 1:12,13; Romans 8:14,15).

The first three petitions refer to God.

First Petition. — "Hallowed be Thy name" (Matthew 6:9). God's name stands also "for His word, His day and His commandments." God's name is hallowed when we think and speak of Him with reverence and love. Any man who speaks of God's name with contempt or takes it in vain at once shows his position in regard to God. The character of a man and of a community is shown by the respect or disrespect in which God's name is held. Hence in praying "Hallowed be Thy name" we pray not only that God may be rightly worshipped but for the upbuilding of the character of men and communities. "Holy, holy, holy, is the Lord of hosts: the whole earth is full of His glory" (Isaiah 6:3; John 17:3; Matthew 5:16; 1 Corinthians 10:31; Exodus 20:7).

Second Petition. — "Thy Kingdom come" (Matthew 6:10). "This is the spiritual kingdom of grace and glory." The supplication is here for the reign of righteousness in all hearts throughout the world; this includes the building up of the home church, and home and foreign missions. It expresses the desire for the conversion of all nations and bringing them under the dominion of our Lord (Revelation 11:15; 1 Corinthians 15:28; Matthew 9:37,38; 6:33; 13:31-33; Luke 17:21).

Third Petition. — "Thy will be done in earth as it is in heaven" (Matthew 6:10). The will of God concerning us is that we should be holy as He is holy (Leviticus 11:44) that we should be perfect as He is perfect (Matthew 5:48) and that we may believe on His Son (John 6:40). In proportion as God's will is done on earth, evil, want, misery, oppression, hate, jealousy, vanity and evil speaking will disappear from the earth. We might then, when His will is done on earth as it is in heaven, shut up our jails, dismiss our police force, close our courts, and reduce taxes to a minimum. When we offer this petition we are asking for large things.

The last three petitions refer to man and his needs.

Fourth Petition. — "Give us this day our daily bread" (Matthew 6:11). This supplication calls our attention to the fact that we are dependent upon God for daily food and that we are to ask Him to supply our bodily wants. Daily bread includes food, raiment and shelter and all that belongs to our temporal necessities. The answer to this prayer may be in health, bodily and mental strength to procure daily bread, but nevertheless it comes from the hand of God and He should be thanked for it as well as asked for it (Deuteronomy 8:10; Psalm 145: 15,16; Proverbs 30:8).

Fifth Petition. — "Forgive us our debts as we forgive our debtors" (Matthew 6:12). The word debts here means sins. In asking for forgiveness of sins, we acknowledge that we have sinned and are in need of forgiveness. We pray the Father to forgive us and seek in this way to be reconciled to Him. But it is through Jesus Christ that the Father forgives men their sins. "Behold the Lamb of God, which taketh away the sin of the world" (John 1:29; 1 John 1:7-9; John 3:16-19; Ephesians 1:7). In repeating the latter clause of the petition, "as we forgive our debtors" we acknowledge that we have not only sinned against God but also against our fellow men and that they have sinned against us and caused us to cherish enmity in our hearts. If we desire God's forgiveness we must forgive our fellow men and be reconciled with them before we can expect to come to God and receive His full forgiveness for our transgressions. "Be not overcome of evil but overcome evil with good" (Romans 12:20,21). "If ye forgive men their trespasses your heavenly Father will also forgive you, but if ye forgive not men their trespasses, neither will your Father forgive your trespasses" (Matthew 6:14,15; 18:21,22; Luke 17:3,4).

Sixth Petition. — "Lead us not into temptation, but deliver us from evil" (Matthew 6:13). In this petition we acknowledge our weakness and proneness to go astray. We seek for God's strong power to guard us from and in all temptations of the flesh and spirit. We ask for final deliverance from the power and effects of all evil. We look forward to an abode with God where no evil can come to us. "The Lord shall deliver me from every evil work and will preserve me unto His heavenly kingdom" (2 Timothy 4:18; Psalm 31:5; 1 Peter 5:8; 1 John 5:4; 2:15; Matthew 26:41; 2 Timothy 4:7,8).

The Doxology. — "For Thine is the kingdom, and the power, and the glory forever. Amen" (Matthew 6:13). This is an ascription of praise showing that in God is vested all power and glory, that there is no kingdom above His kingdom and that He is supreme over all. Before Him must come all things for judgment. He alone is to be worshipped, for in Him is all power and truth and goodness.

"Thine, O Lord, is the greatness, and the power, and the glory, and the victory, and the majesty: for all that is in the heaven and in the earth is Thine; Thine is the kingdom, O Lord, and Thou art exalted as head above all" (1 Chronicles 29:11,12; Psalm 115:1; Ephesians 3:20,21).

ANSWERS TO PRAYER

Nothing could indicate more plainly that God cares for and loves men, and is not indifferent to their wants, than the great stream of prayer flowing through the Bible. He is not a God afar off, neither has He wound up the universe as a great machine and left it to its fate. He is in touch with His people. He hears them when they cry to Him. He is long-suffering, merciful and righteous. Happy is the man who loves God with all his heart and who seeks constantly to commune with Him.

Notable Instances of Prayer, and the response of God, are shown in the following passages of Scripture. Abraham (Genesis 20:17), Jacob (Genesis 32:24-31), Moses (Numbers 11:2), Samuel (1 Samuel 12:18), Elijah (1 Kings 18:37-46), Hezekiah (2 Kings 20:2-6), Ezra (9:5-15), Daniel (9:3-27), Jesus Christ (Matthew 6:6-15; John 17), The Apostles (Acts 1:14; 4:31), Peter (Acts 12:5-11), Paul and Silas (Acts 16:25-32), Prophets and teachers at Antioch (Acts 13:1-3) and Paul and the elders at Ephesus (Acts 20:36).

QUESTIONS

The province of prayer; give a definition of prayer. What are the different kinds and places of prayer? What can be said of the approach of man to God? What is right knowledge of God? Right attitude of heart to God? Right subjects of prayer? What has persistency to do in praying to God? What can be said of the approach of God to man? How does the Bible and Christian experience testify of this approach of God to man? What is the great outside difficulty urged against God's approach to man and what can be said of it? What is the model prayer? Give the divisions of the model prayer and explain them. What can be said of answers to prayer?

STUDY VIII

THE CHRISTIAN SERVICE

Scripture references: Matthew 28:18-20; Luke 10:1-17; Matthew 25:14-30; 23; 13; John 13:4-17; Hebrews 12:1-3; Matthew 5:16; 1 Corinthians 3:13-15; James 2:14-26.

THE CALL TO SERVICE

All Christian belief must culminate in service or else the belief itself will wither away. Jesus said in His Sermon on the Mount, "Let your light so shine before men that they may see your good works and glorify your Father which is in heaven" (Matthew 5:16); again, in giving His parting instructions to His disciples, He commanded, "Go ye therefore and teach all nations" (Matthew 28:19,20). "Faith, if it hath not works, is dead" (James 2:17).

The New Testament rings with an optimistic trumpet call to service; there is not a single pessimistic note sounded. A man expresses his belief and he at once goes to work. To the fact that men were so willing to lead a strenuous Christian life in those early times is due in large measure the marvellous spread of the gospel faith.

The Object of the Call was not a cause but a Person (Acts 1:8; 2:22,36,38; 4:12; 10:43; 16:31); to set forth Jesus Christ as the Saviour of men. The world was full of evil. Society was corrupt. The state was bad. There were many giant wrongs crying out for the reformer. The apostles might have devoted themselves to the causes of social and political reform with splendid success. They might have bought only a gradual and purely friendly approach to the people whom they wished to influence, as we often do now, with some success, but the New Testament writings show that they believed that in the person of Jesus Christ they had a more powerful remedy for bad social and political conditions than any other which they could urge. In Christ they found a supreme object of service; for

Him they were willing to give up houses, lands, position, even life itself (2 Timothy 4:6-8); for only through Him, they preached, could the world be truly reformed. Why then potter with temporary and minor remedies when the permanent and great remedy was at hand? Times have changed since the apostolic days, but for any lasting good in reform work Christ is still the great remedy. He must be at the centre of all social, political and temperance betterments or they are destined to fall short of the largest success.

The Place. — Where shall men serve the Christ?

1. In the heart; there is a goodness of conduct on the part of some men which has no relation to their heart's desire and is simply a cloak worn for appearance's sake. With this sort of goodness Jesus had no sympathy and denounced it as hypocrisy (Matthew 6:1-34; 23:27, 28). Christ's service must commence with an inward conformity to the law of God. This necessity for a new heart is very clearly brought out in His conversation with Nicodemus (John 3:1-21).

2. In the home. Jesus said to a man whom He had healed, "Go home to thy friends, and tell them how great things the Lord hath done for thee" (Mark 5:19). Anything that strengthens the home strengthens society and the state. Good homes are essential for the bringing up of children and the making of right characters. But it is in the home that the real testing often comes of a professed Christianity; if a Christian life can be lived and manifested here it is quite sure to stand the outward strain.

3. In the community. The disciples of Christ were commanded to begin their first service in Jerusalem (Acts 1:4,8), where Jesus had been the most persecuted and was finally crucified. It was no easy task for them to begin to preach Jesus, where they were the most looked down upon. But the command was justified when the day of Pentecost came with the marvellous moving power of the Holy Spirit (Acts 2). There can be no clearer teaching from this than that a Christian man should begin to serve Christ, testify for Him and work for Him in the community in which he resides no matter what the adverse conditions are. Here is the sanction for home missions.

4. Abroad. "Go ye into all the world and preach the gospel to every creature" (Mark 16:15; Matthew 28:18-20). The field of service broadens out from the heart until it takes in the whole world and

every class and condition of men. Man under the guidance of Christ is led not only to think of saving himself, his home, his community, but all homes and communities however remote they may be from his own. Here is the sanction for foreign missions.

The urgency of the call is everywhere manifest in the New Testament. In the three years of His ministry Jesus Christ is incessant in His labours, calling upon men to turn to Him (Matthew 11:28-30). He urges watchfulness, prayerfulness, and earnestness in seeking to enter the kingdom of God (Matthew 11:12; 25:13; 26:41; Mark 14:38; Luke 11:9,10). Paul declared, "Woe is me, if I preach not the gospel" (1 Corinthians 9:16), and he urges Timothy to "preach the word" and to be "instant in season and out of season" (2 Timothy 4:1,2).

A conflict is going on in the world and those who believe in Christ are besought to take every possible opportunity and every means to advance His gospel and cause men to accept Him as their Saviour (Ephesians 6:10-18).

THE PATTERN OF SERVICE

The world of men is frequently more easily moved by the force of example than by precept.

Christ declared Himself to be the great exemplar of the Christian life. He said, "I have given you an example that ye should do as I have done to you" (John 13:15; 12:32; 1 Peter 2:21). He practiced what He preached.

Personal Work.—In winning persons to the new life there is an admitted need of a work of the individual for the individual, but it is a task from which many draw back. Yet it is right here that the most effective service may be accomplished. Every man who receives Christ becomes in a certain sense a trustee to enlist others in His service and to give to them the light of life. Christ said to His followers, "Ye shall be witnesses unto Me" (Acts 1:8).

Jesus was no recluse, He went out amongst men and sought them (Mark 10:45) in the market-place, in the fields and by the lakeside. Everywhere He entered into personal conversation, with those whom He met, about the kingdom of God; now it was with Nicodemus (John 3:1-21), then again with the woman of Samaria (John 4:4-26) and others. This personal work of Christ with individuals shows the importance He attached to the winning of persons one by one to Himself. Many of the most important teachings are brought out in His personal conversations.

"The win one movement" which has been inaugurated in certain churches is very important. It had its incentive in the narrative of John (1:40-51), who tells us how Andrew won Peter and Philip won Nathanael by personal appeals to follow Christ. If all the followers of Christ in all the churches would each win one soul for Christ every year there would be no more complaints about decadent churches.

Training Others for Service. — Personal work has its limitations in the time and strength of the individual who does it. Jesus thoroughly understood this fact and at the outset of His ministry began to train a band of followers who would carry on His work after His resurrection. Not only did He train a select company of twelve but also other men. We read in Luke, the ninth chapter, that He sent out His twelve disciples to do the work which He had been doing, and in the tenth chapter we are told that "other seventy" were also appointed to carry on a similar work. Careful instructions were given the seventy as to what they should do. The need (Luke 10:2) and the danger (v. 3) of the work were impressed upon them. They were instructed how they were to approach the people, what they were to teach and what they were to do in case they were rejected (vs. 4-11). They returned from their journey with great joy over its success (v. 17).

This multiplication of self through the inciting and training of others to do work in which the individual is interested often leads to far-reaching results. There are many people who desire to advance a cause and are willing to devote themselves to it, but they have no power to set about it themselves. There is any quantity of this usable and helpful material, in our churches, ready to be made of service for the Master. Here is the waste that every professing Christian is not set to advance the kingdom of God. It is not only what a Christian may do himself, but what he can get others to do, which counts.

Teaching.—Many men go wrong from erroneous thoughts about God and the importance of a right character. Too frequently those who have come to a saving knowledge of Christ are content to rest satisfied with it. No effort is made to instruct others in a belief which has helped them. The church believes in a teaching ministry, but has not yet come to fully believe in a teaching laity. The laity for the most part assumes a receptive attitude. Our Bible-schools might be doubled in numbers and effectiveness if Christian men and women, well qualified for the task, could be induced to respond to the strong demand for more teachers. There is no reason why Bible instruction and Christian teaching should be wholly confined to Sunday. It is time that the church made an aggressive move upon the week-days and began the establishment of night schools (for a definite term) for the systematic study of the Bible for adults and short after day school catechetical classes for children. These classes could and should be made auxiliary to the Sunday Bible-school. In them there would be time for that larger instruction which is so much needed and for which no opportunity is found under the present arrangement. Besides, much talent not available upon Sunday, at the time of the session of the Bible-school, might be utilized. This is an age of clubs organized for the study of ancient and modern secular literature, where careful and scholarly papers are read upon subjects given out long in advance. This study-club idea ought to be utilized by the church for the investigation of the best literature which the world knows, namely, that found in the Bible.

Jesus said, "Go teach" (Matthew 28:19,20), and He Himself taught the people in large and small groups (Matthew 5:1,2), on a mountain, in the synagogue (Matthew 4:23; Mark 1:21), by the seaside (Mark 2:13), in the temple (Matthew 26:55), as He walked through the fields and when He went to feasts and social gatherings. He had ever in mind His teaching mission. He set an example of persistent and painstaking instruction of the people under bitter opposition and in adverse circumstances. He said, in encouraging His disciples to persevere in their teaching, "Remember the word that I said unto you, the servant is not greater than his Lord. If they have persecuted Me they will also persecute you; if they have kept My saying they will keep yours also" (John 15:20).

Works of Mercy and Love.—Jesus was the supreme embodiment of mercy and love. Possessed of almighty power He used it not for honour or for selfish purposes, but to heal and help men (Matthew 11:5; 9:36; 14:14; 15:32; 20:34; Mark 1:41; 6:34; Luke 7:13). Modern philanthropy had its origin in Him. All the modern state institutions for the care of the poor, the blind, the crippled, the sick are in existence to-day because of the teaching and example of Jesus Christ. Before He came to earth and taught men how to be compassionate towards the unfortunate ones there were no such institutions.

Wherever Jesus went, when He was in bodily form upon this earth, the people thronged Him for the healing touch. This is another way in which the followers of Christ may reach men, namely through the healing touch. In the fierce struggle in the world, for a living and a position, many men are worsted and trampled upon; such men need the brotherly help of those who have been with Christ. There are many sick, discouraged and poor; here is a large field for this service of mercy and love.

Suffering.—There is a ministry of suffering in taking and bearing the burdens of others. "For it became Him (Christ), for whom are all things and by whom are all things, in bringing many sons unto glory, to make the captain of their salvation perfect through suffering" (Hebrews 2:10). This suffering of Christ is represented by the New Testament writers as having an object in the salvation of man and bringing him to glory (Romans 8:18; 2 Corinthians 1:5-7; Hebrews 2:9; 1 Peter 1:11; 4:13; 5:1; Philippians 3:10).

Isaiah said of Christ, "He was wounded for our transgressions, He was bruised for our iniquities: the chastisement of our peace was upon Him; and with His stripes we are healed" (Isaiah 53:5). We are urged to follow the example set by Christ (Philippians 2:5-11) in His humility and suffering for a great purpose. "In every age Christ's sufferings attract to Him the hearts of men; for they prove the boundless extent of His love, His absolute unselfishness, and His loyalty to truth and principle even unto death. Thus they have power with men." In following Christ, and placing Him in a right light before men, Christians must have a devotion to Him which will endure and stand steadfast through suffering. It is often only through the sacrifice of self that the best things in life are attained.

"If so be we suffer with Him that we may be also glorified together. For I reckon that the sufferings of the present time are not worthy to be compared with the glory which shall be revealed in us" (Romans 8:17,18).

THE JOY OF SERVICE

Jesus is represented as doing His work through love (John 3:16), and for the joy that was set before Him (Hebrews 12:2).

The Search for Happiness. — How can I be happy? This is the great question with multitudes of people. Men seek joy with the same eagerness that they dig for gold. Yet this world is a sad one, full of care, sickness, anxiety and sorrow. Many are the railers at fate and circumstances which keep them from realizing the object of their search.

The failure to find happiness arises in large part from going wrongly about it. Men seek happiness through relaxation and the lowering of the moral standards. Men ask, why should we obey this or that law of God, man or our moral nature, if it bars the way to our enjoyment? "Let us eat and drink for to-morrow we die"; and eating and drinking they go out into a wild and barren land of sorrow. Again men seek happiness through the abundance of things; as if a human soul, born in the image of God, could be satisfied with mere things.

The Conditions of Christian Happiness. — Christ, as the Great Pattern of life, showed that true happiness must be attained through the mastery of the situation, the victory over temptation (Matthew 4:1-11), and the hardest and most adverse circumstances of life (Hebrews 12:3; Philippians 2:8-10; 2:1,2; Matthew 16:21-27). There is no greater joy than that of the victors in a hard fought battle. Heaven is for conquerors (Revelation 15:2,3; 17:14). It is the man who has gone down into the tumult and uproar of the arena of life and fought and conquered in some good cause who tastes the supreme cup of happiness. The master words of the Christ were, "fight," "watch," "pray"; here is the entrance to the Utopia so long sought by men. The man who has no control over his appetites, passions and temper, and who cannot endure hardness in a service in which he is interested, can never know what genuine joy is. Read the roll call of the heroes in the eleventh chapter of Hebrews.

1. A great object in view. There can be no greater object than to serve Christ in all the relations of life (Matthew 6:33; 10:38; 8:22; 16:24; 19:21).

2. Harmony with the will of God (Matthew 6:10).

3. Endurance. Paul exhorts Timothy, "Thou therefore my son, be strong in the grace that is in Christ Jesus. And the things that thou hast heard of me among many witnesses, the same commit thou to faithful men, who shall be able to teach others also. Thou therefore endure hardness, as a good soldier of Jesus Christ" (2 Timothy 2:1-3). It was this quality of endurance in service which Jesus sought to set before His followers in the strongest light (Matthew 10:22; 24:13).

Here then are the elements of the greatest human happiness and a divine joy. It is only as the human heart is thus prepared for the reception of the enlightenment of the Holy Spirit that He can be received in His glory, which He desires to impart to men and to bring them into joyous fellowship with the Father and the Son.

QUESTIONS

What is the call to service? What is the object of the call? Where shall men serve the Christ? How shall men serve the Christ in the heart, home, community, abroad? What can be said of the urgency of the call to service? What is the pattern of service? What can be said of personal work, training others for service, teaching, works of mercy and love, suffering? What is the joy of service? What can be said of the search for happiness? What are the conditions of Christian happiness in service?

STUDY IX

THE CHRISTIAN CHURCH

Scriptures references: 1 Corinthians 3:11; 3:6-9; Colossians 1:18; Acts 2:47; Ephesians 5:23-27; Matthew 16:16,18; 18:17; Acts 5:11,12; 13:1,2; 14:23; 16:5; 1 Corinthians 11:18-34; 12:28-31; 1 Thessalonians 1:1; 2:14; 1 Timothy 3:15; Hebrews 12:22,23; Revelation 1:4,11,20; 2:7,11; 22:16; 22:12-15,17.

THE FOUNDATION OF THE CHURCH

What is the Christian Church?—One of the best definitions is as follows: "The church consists of all who acknowledge the Divine Lord, Jesus Christ, the blessed Saviour of mankind, who give credit to His gospel, and who hold His sacraments, the seals of eternal life, in honour." Another definition is: "The church is a holy kingdom established by God on earth, of which Christ is the invisible King." There are some organizations calling themselves Christian churches which have substituted certain philosophical doctrines in place of the principles of Jesus Christ, but it is a fact of history that in proportion as the Divine Lordship of Christ has been exalted the greater has been the growth of the church. The church has been able to meet the needs of the people as He has been lifted up (John 12:32) that men might turn to Him for light and life (John 1:4; 8:12; 12:46; Matthew 11:27-30).

The Head of the Church is Jesus Christ. When Simon Peter made the declaration, "Thou art the Christ the Son of the living God," Jesus said unto him, "Blessed art thou, Simon Barjona: for flesh and blood hath not revealed it unto thee, but My Father which is in heaven. And I say unto thee, That thou art Peter, and upon this rock I will build My church" (Matthew 16:16-18; Ephesians 2:20). "The question is, What is this rock? The Romanists say, 'It is Peter'; but Christ did not so say. His statement was, 'Thou art Petros and on this petra I will build My church.' The words are cognate but not identical; the former is masculine and the latter feminine; petra is a rock; Petros is a stone hewn out of the rock." When Christ uttered these words He was on His way to Jerusalem where He was to be crucified. In the face of the cross, the Master was preparing His disciples for a great trial and the time when, in bodily presence, He should depart from the earth. It was necessary that He should now speak plainly in regard to Himself and His mission.

Paul, in writing to the Colossians, said of Christ, "And He is the head of the body, the church: who is the beginning, the first-born from the dead; that in all things He might have the preeminence" (Colossians 1:18; compare Ephesians 1:22,23).

However Christian churches may differ from each other in form of government and in other matters they are united in the great essential doctrine of the Headship of Christ, this is their strong bond of union.

A Divine Institution. — The Christian church was not organized by any one man or a company of men, but was given to man as an expression of the compassion of God (John 3:16-21), that in it men might associate themselves together for the proper worship of God and that they might draw near to Him (Hebrews 10:19-25).

1. The beginning of the organization of the church was in the upper room, where Jesus partook of the last supper with His disciples (Matthew 26:20-30). Here He showed the significance of His death (v. 28), His relation to the Father (John 14:9), and the coming of the Holy Spirit (John 14:16,17; 15:26,27). In the last instructions given by Jesus, and His prayer (John 14:1-17:26) we have a body of teaching which constitutes the basis of the faith of the church.

2. The completion of the organization of the church was in the descent of the Holy Spirit upon the day of Pentecost (Acts 2:1-24,32,36-41), which the disciples had been commanded to await in the city of Jerusalem (Acts 1:6-8,14). Those who accepted the word which had been preached through the Holy Spirit were baptized (2:41). "The Lord," not men, "added to the church daily such as should be saved" (Acts 2:47).

Ordinances and Faith.—The church, with its ordinances of the Lord's
Supper and Baptism, its faith in God the Father, in His Son Jesus
Christ and in the Holy Spirit, now begins its victorious career.

Human Elements.—The divine institution of the church has been
subject to the admixture of human elements, there was a traitor
amongst the twelve apostles. The organization and the doctrines
have been tampered with in the interest of human ambitions and
the pride of human philosophy, but no institution has shown itself
so adapted to satisfy the great needs of men of all conditions of life,
to purge itself when the human elements proved too great a burden,
and to outlast all man-made organizations.

Authority and Teaching.—The church and its ministers have authority to teach through Christ and what He has commanded. There
is a certain and quite definite body of truth. This body of truth,
preached in the heart of heathendom or in the most fashionable
church, in the most highly civilized country, is quite sure to produce
certain definite results in awakening men from their sins and caus-
ing them to lead a new life. "By their fruits ye shall know them"
(Matthew 7:15-20).

Jesus said, "All power is given unto Me in heaven and in earth.
Go ye therefore and teach all nations, baptizing them in the name of
the Father, and of the Son and of the Holy Ghost. Teaching them to
observe all things whatsoever I have commanded you and lo I am
with you alway, even unto the end of the world" (Matthew 28:18-20;
Luke 10:22; John 3:35; 5:32; 13:3; 17:2; Acts 2:36; Romans 14:9).

Paul said, "For other foundation can no man lay than that is laid,
which is Jesus Christ" (1 Corinthians 3:11).

Form.—The word church, in the New Testament, is used in three
senses to denote the differences in the form.

1. The local congregation worshipping in a house (Philemon 2;
Colossians 4:15) or a certain place as, "The church of God which is at
Corinth" (1 Corinthians 1:2) and "the church of the Thessalonians" (1
Thessalonians 1:1). This is much the most frequent use of the word.

2. The entire community of Christians throughout the world or some portions of it (1 Corinthians 15:9; Galatians 1:13; Matthew 16:18).

3. The total company of the redeemed, the bride of Christ (Ephesians 5:23,25,27,30; Hebrews 12:23).

The Life of the Early Church, as we have seen, had its origin in Jesus Christ. Those who came into the church, did so because of their belief in Him and acceptance of Him as their Saviour.

1. The organization was simple; each church looked to Christ as its head (1 Corinthians 1:2-18,30; Ephesians 5:23).

2. The officers were appointed for certain necessary duties (Acts 6;20:17-23; Titus 1:5-7); it was the Lord who called men into certain vocations for the edifying of the church (Ephesians 4:11,12; 1 Corinthians 12:27,28).

3. The time of meeting was upon the first day of the week (Acts 20:7; 1 Corinthians 16:2), thus commemorating the resurrection of the Lord (John 20:1,19; Luke 24:1; Mark 16:2; Matthew 28:1).

4. The aim was to build up pure and godly lives (Titus 2:1-15) and to bring all men into fellowship with the Master. There was an intense enthusiasm for the faith and propagation of it. There was an extraordinary religious elevation and purity of conduct. The churches set themselves to eradicate the selfishness in man, out of which all forms of injustice sprang and aimed to affect the moral renovation of the individual and of society. There were abuses which arose out of the former lives of believers; it is surprising, considering the evil influences surrounding the early churches, that they were so few.

5. But there arose in the midst of a gross heathenism, with all its great immoralities, a rapidly growing community, which demanded purity of life and conduct from its communicants and supreme allegiance to Christ, the Lord and Saviour; how strong it was is shown by the fact that the Roman Empire tried to stamp it out, failed, and was taken captive itself by the religion it had despised.

THE WORK OF THE MODERN CHURCH

The Chief End of the Church is to carry on the work which brought Christ into the world (Luke 19:10; 17:33; 15:1-24; 24:48; Acts 1:8). All things should be made to serve this purpose.

The Activities and methods of work have a wide range. What is highly successful in one community may prove, however, a failure in another. The means, which produce large results at one time, tried again in the same place, at another time, sometimes show small or no results.

The problem of each church and community needs to be studied, that means may be properly adjusted and adapted to the ends sought to be accomplished. It is remarkable how Jesus adapted Himself to the times and circumstances. He said to Peter and Andrew, "Follow Me and I will make you fishers of men" (Matthew 4:19); He spoke to them in a language they were able to comprehend; to fish for fish meant care, understanding of their habits and much toil to accomplish the desired results. In the conversations with Nicodemus and the women of Samaria Jesus arrives at the same end but uses entirely different means. The letters of Paul fit exactly the needs of the churches to which they are addressed.

It is the really earnest spirit desiring to bring men to Christ which will produce the largest results; this spirit appeals to men and compels them to listen; hence it is the cultivation of this spirit which is most earnestly commended. Mere machinery of effort is doomed to failure, but when the living spirit is in the wheels and is adequate to the moving of them, the results are sure to be large. The disciples of Christ knew all the facts about Christ's life, death and resurrection, but they were not equipped for their great work until after they had spent much time in prayer and the Holy Spirit had come in power; then they became mighty men in the upbuilding of the church.

Worship. — "Men not only need to be urged to be true to their consciences, but their consciences need to be informed." One of the great functions of the church is to teach men how to worship God aright; to do this they must have right thoughts about God. Jesus said, "God is a Spirit: and they that worship Him must worship Him in spirit and in truth" (John 4:24). Men must be led in their worship by a proper exposition of the Scriptures, by prayer and by praise.

The place of the church in this matter is clearly defined in the New Testament, it can be taken by no other institution; and no other organization has so high a mission as this, to bring man into harmony with God.

Fellowship.—Man is a social being and he seeks contact with his fellow men. Many of the worldly ways in which this fellowship is sought are ways which lead to the wrecking of man, body and soul, or to the obliteration of all the finer feelings. The mission of the Christian Church is to strengthen the social bond by seeking to cultivate all the better impulses and finer feelings in man, and to place society on a firmer footing in love, purity and righteousness (1 John 1:3; 1:5; Acts 2:42; 1 Corinthians 1:9).

Bible Study.—Christianity is a book religion as well as one in which God enters into spiritual communion with man. The Church has ever acknowledged its duty to teach the Scriptures, for in them it finds the truths which it desires to inculcate (John 5:39).

Evangelization.—Beyond the bounds of the Church there are those, near and far away, who need to be taught about the gospel of Jesus Christ. More and more the church is feeling the responsibility for the welfare of individuals and of society and of the state. If there are great evils and giant wrongs which need to be remedied, they have their origin in the evil in men's hearts. For the cure of bad hearts there is no remedy in all the world save that given by Jesus Christ. Hence the activity of the church in seeking to evangelize men not only at home but throughout the world.

There are three things which every church needs to realize in order that this work may be prosecuted with the utmost vigour and enthusiasm.

1. A clear conception of what the church is and its relations to God and man.

2. The opening of the eyes to the fact of sin in the world and its destructive power upon the soul of man, here and hereafter (1 John 1:8; Romans 5:12; John 8:34; Matthew 18:7-11).

3. That the only real help or salvation of man's soul is through our Divine Lord and Saviour, Jesus Christ. "Neither is there salvation in any other: for there is none other name under heaven given among

men, whereby we must be saved" (Acts 4:12; 16:30,31; Philippians 2:10; 1 John 2:12; Romans 10:13; 1 John 1:7,9; Matthew 9:6).

The Equipment for the carrying on and extension of this work cannot be too good. The cause frequently lags from making it one of the interests of life and not the chief care. Every church building should express in usefulness and beauty, in all its appointments, man's thought of a temple erected to the great and living God.

THE HOPE OF THE CHURCH

The Establishment of the Kingdom of God Upon Earth.—The prophets of the Old Testament had two great thoughts which they continually presented, namely, the coming of the Messianic King and the establishment of the Messianic kingdom. Isaiah said, "Unto us a Child is born, unto us a Son is given: and the government shall be upon His shoulder and He shall be called Wonderful, Counsellor, The Mighty God, The Everlasting Father, The Prince of Peace. Of the increase of His government and peace there shall be no end" (9:6,7).

When John the Baptist came, he proclaimed the coming of this King and kingdom (Matthew 3:11,12; John 1:1-28) and when he saw Jesus he said, "Behold the Lamb of God which taketh away the sin of the world. This is He of whom I said, After me cometh a man who is preferred before me: for He was before me" (John 1:29-33). "And I saw and bare record that this is the Son of God" (v. 34).

Jesus spoke much about His kingdom, the kingdom of heaven and the kingdom of God. He sought to explain by many parables and by direct discourse what this kingdom was like; it is mentioned by name many times in the New Testament (Matthew 13:11,19,24,31,33,44,45,47, 52; 22:2; 25:1). He claimed that He was the Messianic King (Matthew 26:63,64; 27:11,37; 26:53,54; 16:16,17; John 14:9; Luke 22:67,69; John 18:37; Mark 14:61,62), and the Son of God. He declared that before Him all nations should come to be judged (Matthew 25:31-46). As in the Old Testament so in the New Testament the world-wide character of this kingdom of God is plainly shown.

There are Four Conceptions of the Kingdom of God set forth in the Bible. 1. The reign of God over all His creatures. 2. The reign of God over men and nations. 3. The reign of God over Israel. 4. "The reign of God as Divine Love over human hearts, believing in Him and constrained thereby to yield Him grateful affection and devoted love." It is this fourth conception which is most prominently set forth in the New Testament. The special work of Christ on earth was to reveal the supreme rule of Divine Love.

The Church and the Kingdom.—It is the care of the church to forward the establishment of this kingdom of Divine Love everywhere, in the heart of the individual, in society, in the business world and in the national life. For this we pray, as Christ taught us, "Thy kingdom come. Thy will be done in earth, as it is in heaven" (Matthew 6:10).

QUESTIONS

What is the Christian Church? Define it. Who is the Head of the church? How is the church a divine institution? What can be said of the beginning and completion of the organization? What are the ordinances? What can be said of the human elements? Where is the authority and ground of teaching? What can be said of the forms? What can be said of the life of the early church? What is the chief end of the church? What can be said of the activities of the modern church? What of the worship? What of the fellowship? What three things are necessary to keep clearly in mind, in the work of evangelization? What ought the church equipment to be? What is the hope of the church? What are the four conceptions of the Kingdom of God? What is the chief conception? What can be said of the church and the kingdom?

STUDY X

THE CHRISTIAN HOME

Scripture references: Ephesians 6:1-9; 5:25-33; Colossians 3:17-25; 1 Corinthians 7:12-17; Mark 10:2-12; 7:9-13; 5:19; 1 Timothy 5:4; Luke 15:6; Titus 2:1-15; Exodus 20:12,17; Deuteronomy 6:1-9.

THE HOME

What is a Home? — It has been answered that, "It is the unit of society." It has also been pointed out that this unit must be kept clean, pure and right, in all its relations, or society and the state will suffer grave consequences. Certainly, in the past, the institutions of society and state have been seriously weakened only when the moral decay of the family has first set in. There are many organizations which have for their special care the fostering of the social and political life, while the strengthening of home ties has been sadly neglected.

To the individual the good character of the home is of the utmost importance, for his growth in all the finer things which pertain to morality and spirituality.

The Difference in Homes. — One ideal of a home begins and ends with the externals; a great house, a splendid service and fine furnishings. Everything is here made to bend to the more or less perfect realization of this material ideal. When all is attained that is possible in this direction, and this end, and only this end, is sought of outer adornment, it is found that the essentials of a true home life have been missed.

Another ideal seeks for the cultivation of love between husband and wife, and all the members of the family. Care and forbearance are urged and commended in speech and action. There are set forth a mutual kindness, a careful consideration of the feelings and a helpfulness in bearing burdens, which exalt the soul and make life worth living. According as this ideal is striven for, and attained, will the true home be realized.

Many a man has wrecked his business, betrayed his friends and gone down to a dishonoured grave in the struggle to surround his family with luxuries which he could not afford, but no man ever sincerely tried to cultivate the graces of love and kindness in himself and in his family, who did not succeed, in a large measure, in realizing the great purpose of the home.

The True Home may be found, and is found, in great houses and in small houses, where there is large wealth and where there is dire poverty. It is not dependent upon circumstances but independent.

The great essential is love for those things which make a beautiful and strong character. Low standards of truth and morality in the family tend to reproduce themselves in exaggerated forms in the social life of the community. Individuals, coming out of families where there is no love for the good and no regard for righteousness, often become a serious threat to peace and good order. No educational system can do very much for children with an evil family environment. On the other hand the world is full of examples of men, trained up in righteousness by their parents, who have strictly kept to the path in which their feet were started.

THE IDEAL CHRISTIAN HOME

Jesus honoured the home. His birthplace was mean (Luke 2:7) so far as external things go. The house and the city, where His parents lived, showed plainly the poor estate of the family which, while it was of noble lineage, was greatly reduced in circumstances. Jesus Himself learned and practiced the trade of a carpenter. In living in this home at Nazareth for thirty years of His life Jesus showed that it was possible under hard outward conditions to live a noble life and to cultivate and practice those virtues and qualities which were afterwards so greatly to bless the whole world.

Duties of Husbands and Wives.—The beginning of every Christian home is in a supreme affection between two, a man and a woman. "For this cause," Christ said, "shall a man leave his father and mother, and cleave to his wife; and they twain shall be one flesh, so that they are no more twain but one flesh. What therefore God hath joined together, let not man put asunder" (Mark 10:7-9). He honoured and sanctioned the marriage relation by His presence at the marriage in Cana (John 2:1-11). In the first century divorce was very common; Hillel, the Jewish teacher, held "that the bond was so loose and flexible that if a wife burnt her husband's food while cooking it, he was justified in procuring a writ of divorcement from her." Jesus denounces this practice and declares (Matthew 5:31,32; Mark 10:2-12) that there is only one cause that justifies divorce.

1. Love to one another. In the various vicissitudes of married life, and in the bringing up of children the bond which needs to be strengthened, and the duty which needs to be urged, is that of love. Love can alone carry husband and wife over the more difficult places of life. Paul says, "Husbands love your wives, even as Christ also loved the Church and gave Himself for it" (Ephesians 5:25-33; Colossians 3:18,19). "Let every one of you so love his wife even as himself; and the wife see that she reverence her husband" (Ephesians 5:33). No stronger language can be employed than Paul uses in urging husband and wife to love each other with a whole heart, yet he provides for cases where one or the other party in the married relation is not a Christian, and where a strong love may be absent (1 Corinthians 7:12-17). He further says, "Unto the married I command, yet not I, but the Lord, let not the wife depart from her husband; but and if she depart let her remain unmarried, or be reconciled to her husband: and let not the husband put away his wife" (1 Corinthians 7: 10,11). But a supreme love settles all troubles (1 Corinthians, chapter 13).

2. Forbearance and kindness towards children. "Provoke not your children to wrath but bring them up in the nurture and admonition of the Lord" (Ephesians 6:4; Colossians 3:21). When Christ was upon earth, "a father had the power of life and death over his offspring. A weak and sickly child might be abandoned to death; and this was approved by such eminent authorities as Plato and Aristotle." Jesus declared for the rights of the children. He not only opened His arms for them, but He gave them a new standing in the world (Mark 10: 14-16; Matthew 18:5). He said, "See that ye despise not one of these

little ones; for in heaven their angels do always behold the face of My Father, which is in heaven." (Matthew 18:10).

3. Hospitality. True Christian love will extend itself beyond the bounds of the household, and seek to do those outside of it good by drawing them within its charmed circle. This hospitality should be given not only to those who can return it again, but also to those from whom no return can ever be expected (Matthew 5:46). "Use hospitality one to another without grudging" (1 Peter 4:9; 1 Timothy 3:2; Titus 1:8; Hebrews 13:2). "But when thou makest a feast, call the poor, the maimed, the lame, the blind: and thou shalt be blessed; for they cannot recompense thee: for thou shalt be recompensed at the resurrection of the just" (Luke 14:13,14,11,12; compare Matthew 25:35,42). In the midst of our splendid charitable boards, which do such a needed work, individual charity and hospitality should not be forgotten and put out of its rightful place.

4. Commending the home to God. In writing to Timothy (2 Timothy 1:5) Paul calls to mind the unfeigned faith that is in Timothy, which dwelt first in his grandmother Lois and then in his mother Eunice. Paul himself was brought up by devout parents. The Bible has many instances of men, like that of Samuel, who have been trained for great parts in the world in a religious household. The old proverb has it, "Like father, like son." If God is honoured by the parents and the home commended to Him, the children will be quite sure to honour Him also. Bring up your children "in the nurture and admonition of the Lord" (Ephesians 6:4). Have them ready to meet Christ at any time (Mark 13:34-37).

Duties of Children.—1. Honouring parents. "Children obey your parents in the Lord, for this is right" (Ephesians 6:1,2,3; compare Exodus 20:12; Colossians 3:20). The first necessary lesson in every human life is to learn the lesson of obedience; if this is not well studied and practiced in the home, the child, when he grows up and goes out for himself, will be quite sure to have a hard time of it and receive some severe buffetings. Those who break the laws of society and the state are those who have first broken the commandment to honour father and mother.

2. Care of parents. Children, when grown up, are sometimes apt to forget the love and care bestowed upon them when they were

young. Their parents become old and feeble and are often unable to look out for themselves. In Jesus' time there was a bad custom of repudiating parents who for any cause needed to be helped. The children had only to say "Corban," that is, that their goods were dedicated to a sacred purpose, to secure release from their filial obligations. Christ denounced this custom in the strongest terms and declared that the children ought to honour their parents by caring for them. Thus He became an advocate for the rights of parents as He had of the rights of children (Mark 7: n, 7-13; Matthew 15:3-6). When in His last agony, on the cross, Jesus provided a home for His mother (John 19:26,27).

Duties of Dependents and Servants. — Jesus commended the honourableness of service. He washed the disciples' feet (John 13:4-16) and then told them that He had given them an example of the kind of service which they should render to each other. He took upon Himself the form of a servant, hiding His glory, that He might accomplish His great work (Philippians 2:6-9). Paul exhorted servants of the household to be obedient, serving, "not with eye service, as men pleasers; but as servants of Christ, doing the will of God from the heart" (Ephesians 6:5-8; Colossians 3:22-25; 1 Corinthians 9:19). Masters are told to be just towards their servants, remembering that they have a Master in heaven (Colossians 4:1). When the runaway slave, Onesimus, is sent back to his master, by Paul, he is commended to Philemon as a brother beloved (Philemon 16). We should hear but little of strikes and lockouts if employers and employees would only take these principles, laid down in the New Testament, for the guidance of masters and servants, for their rules of conduct towards each other and seek to carry them out.

Duties of Young and Old. — "That the aged men be sober, grave, temperate, sound in faith, in charity, in patience. The aged women likewise, that they be in behaviour as becometh holiness, not false accusers, not given to much wine, teachers of good things; that they may teach the young women to be sober, to love their husbands, to love their children, to be discreet, chaste, keepers at home, good, obedient to their own husbands that the word of God be not blasphemed. Young men likewise exhort to the sober minded" (Titus 2:2-6).

THE ATTACK UPON THE HOME

There are many influences at work which seek to minimize the importance of the home life and to undermine it.

There are four quite well defined lines of the attack upon the life of the family.

The Assault Upon the Marriage Relation.—The moral leper advocates that marriage be dissolvable at will, not by mutual consent alone, but when either party to the contract desires its conclusion. The church, in its different branches, stands as a unit against this iniquitous proposition. But how far the civil power has yielded, by the pressure which has been brought to bear, is made manifest by the fact that in the different states of the Union there are now recognized by the courts forty-six legal causes of annulling a marriage. Our courts are crowded with divorce cases and the suits which grow out of them in regard to property and the care of children. That the odour of scandal, going up from such cases is bad, is unquestioned. That the influence, of such proceedings upon the morals of the country, is evil is also sadly admitted. A blow struck at marriage is one which is felt not only by the family but by society and the state. The fall of the Roman empire was preceded by an extraordinary laxness of the marriage tie. It is time the church bestirred itself to oppose more strongly the theory and practice of the moral leper.

The Assault Upon the Quiet of the Home.—In the modern stress and strain of life there is need of a quiet place in which to rest, to get acquainted with God, to know one's family, to live to the best things and to get ready again to engage enthusiastically in the daily battle of life. The home is designed to furnish such a place of rest, when the work of the day is done; it is here, in a Christian home, that there should be an atmosphere of supreme love and care. It is, however, when night comes that all the attractions, which appeal to the love of excitement, put forth their most strenuous efforts to draw to them the inmates of the home. There are amusements and amusements; a person, however, who looks only to be amused seeks by and by those of the strongest flavour and those which border very closely on the forbidden land. The love of excitement grows upon what it feeds and soon, to the habitual pleasure-seeker, the quiet atmosphere and love of the home no longer appeal; he has begun a chase for excitement and pleasure which will never satisfy him. Multitudes of wrecked homes and burned out characters, show the disastrous work of this assault upon the quiet of the home.

The Assault Upon the Purity of the Body.—We are told by Paul that our bodies are temples of God and members of Christ and therefore they should be kept pure and clean (1 Corinthians 3:16,17; 6:15,16). Yet a certain class of so-called reformers are seeking to teach men that to sit in a saloon drinking the beverages there served out, and which defile the purity of the body, makes for manhood.

The modern saloon, which destroys the purity of the body, is one of the most successful of all agencies for the demoralization and the destruction of the home. Once it has fastened its hold upon a man, the time which he should spend with his family is spent in defiling his body in this place; the money which should be spent, in clothing and feeding his wife and children, is squandered here; until the home loses its hold upon him and he selfishly indulges his appetite, no matter who suffers. We are faced with actual conditions and no substitutes of better kept saloons or purer beverages can help very much. It is a travesty of the truth to call a saloon a working men's club; it is his destruction. What is actually needed is a reform which will send men, who frequent saloons back to their homes. The real problem is not how to reform the saloon, but how to make the home better so that father, mother and the children may take delight in spending their evenings there. The policy of some social organizations, which work in the slums of our great cities, seems to be by providing great public dance halls and fostering the saloons to draw the people still further away from the home life and to make it harder to maintain it.

After all the only real remedy for the saloon habit is Christianity. It is only when Christ comes into the heart of a man that he begins to care for his home and to spend his evenings there. The Church, then as possessing the lure for the home, ought to take more seriously to this work in the slums. But the trouble is that the slums do not receive very pleasantly those who seek to cleanse their hearts and bodies, but they do take kindly to the agencies, and often throng them, which look kindly on those things which really keep them down, and insure them miserable homes. Still it remains true that the teaching of Christianity, even when received with hostility, is the only leavening power for better things in the slums. It is one of the hard things to cleanse a man's body before his heart is made clean, but let his heart be purified, and the purity of the body will follow; then the first thought of that man will be for his home and its betterment.

The Assault of Freedom of Speech.—In no place is there more need of kindliness of speech and manner than in the home, yet in no other place is there more plain speaking. The mask of pleasantness, which may be worn all day in business or social relations, may be in the home laid aside; and the character revealed and the vigour of language used may easily drive away every vestige of happiness. When people live together under the same roof the feelings become very tender and are easily hurt. What is said outside may be thought little of, but in the home it is different. "Take us the foxes, the little foxes that spoil the vines: for our vines have tender grapes" (Song of Solomon 2:15).

Incompatibility of temper is a reason sometimes given for the breaking up of a home, but the real reason is an undue familiarity and freedom of speech. Because persons live together in families there should be no license to say everything and anything, no matter who is hurt.

Home happiness is a tender plant, it needs much care and watching, but when it blooms the flowers are of a rare beauty of form and their fragrance exceeds that of all others.

THE PRESERVATION OF THE HOME

How may the home be preserved and made to serve its great end? There are three ways, amongst a greater number, which are here indicated.

Personal Care.—All betterment of the home must begin with the individual and every individual has a chance to exercise this care as his lot is cast in some family. Thought, time, money, all need to be employed in working out in a practical way the ideal of the true home.

Placing the Home Under the Care of God. — There is a need of the reinstatement of the custom of family worship; the place and time where and when the family is commended to God and placed under His care. As children of the great household of God we need constantly to keep in touch with our Father.

The Obedience of the Golden Rule, as it is stated in a new form: I will not do unto others that which I would not have them do to me.
I
will not think of others that which I would not have them think of me.
I will not say of others that which I would not have them say of me.

QUESTIONS

What is a home? What is the difference in homes? What is the true home? What can be said of the ideal Christian home? Duties of husbands and wives; what are the four lines? Duties of children; what are the two lines? What are the duties of servants and dependents; of the young and aged? What can be said of the attack upon the home; the marriage relation, the quiet of the home, the purity of the body, freedom of speech? In what three ways may the home be preserved?

STUDY XI

THE CHRISTIAN BUSINESS WORLD

Scripture references: Proverbs 22:29; Romans 12:11; Psalms 24:1; 50:10-12; Haggai 2:8; Psalm 49:6,10,16,17; 62:10; Matthew 13:22; Mark 10:23,24; Job 31:24-26; Proverbs 3:9; Matthew 25:14-30; 24:45-51; 6:19-21; Luke 12:16-21.

THE IDEAL IN THE BUSINESS WORLD

There is often a wide difference between the methods actually employed in doing business and when they should be. Good men who are in the thick of the battle of competition and rivalry with other firms in the same line of trade, are the quickest to admit this fact. They would gladly see things managed so that every employee should be satisfied with his wages and hours of work and every competitor and customer gratified by the treatment he receives.

Business as a Fight. — "The truth is," says a recent eminent writer on this subject, "modern business is a fight. At bottom it is a question of strength and courage." In this fight there are all sorts of men engaged; men, who are honourable and upright and who fight fairly, taking no mean advantage, yet nevertheless fighting strongly for place, power and wealth. Over against this company of men are those who are fair only when they are compelled to be fair and who contend with any means, good or bad, for the objects which they seek to attain. It is this latter class which upsets trade, causes great commercial and banking houses to fail, and casts suspicion upon all corporations, by the sale of watered and fraudulent stocks. It is this idea of business as a struggle which causes working men to strike sometimes rightly, against great abuses, and sometimes wrongly, over minor matters which might easily have been adjusted if they had been taken up in the right way.

Business as a Service.—So long as the ideal of the business world is that business is a fight, little can be done to improve the present conditions under which capital and labour work and suffer. There is nothing which is so costly as war, nothing which is so far-reaching in its disastrous effects and which leaves such a trail of misery behind it. Industrial war is no exception to the rule.

But why look upon business as a fight? Already a new ideal is before the world, that of service. This is what business really is, it carries things from the place where they are abundant to where they are not, it seeks to feed, to clothe, to house all mankind and to facilitate travel and commerce. Upon the earth, and in it, enough of all things has been provided for all the inhabitants—the table spread by God has been bountifully furnished—if only there were a proper distribution no one need want. It is this matter of unwillingness to unselfishly serve others which slows down commerce to-day. When, however, men shall cast aside all other ideals save that of being of the largest service to their fellow men we shall have a new order of things. Men will no longer seek to accumulate for themselves alone and the labourer will work with his full strength and a glad enthusiasm.

No man ever did his best work without some great ideal before him which refreshed and quickened all his energies. If the business man would save himself from becoming sordid, and the poorest paid working man from becoming sullen and hardened, they should keep ever before them this vision of service.

OWNERSHIP

If the ideal of service is accepted in the business world as true, then the question arises, What or whom shall man serve? Shall it be a thing, silver, gold, house or land? Shall a man serve another man as a man? Whatsoever a man serves he becomes subject to. He is dominated by it and his thoughts go no further. Every man is tempted to serve the lower instead of the higher. Jesus was tempted (Matthew 4:1-11) by certain seeming great and temporal advantages to relinquish His service of His Father, but He made it clear once and for all that the supreme object of service should be God (Matthew 4:10), "Him only shalt thou serve." Paul also exhorts all men, in all occupations, to keep in mind first of all the service of God and of Christ, and to do whatever they do to God. Then if they administer great or small affairs, if they are masters or servants, they will seek to please God and, having this higher ideal, will do far better work, than they otherwise would, in every sphere of life (Ephesians 6:7; Colossians 3:17,23; 1 Corinthians 10:31; 2 Corinthians 8:5).

God, the Owner of All. — God as sovereign, and over and in all, is the proper object of service (Exodus 20:3,4,5) for the business man. Nations have parceled out the earth amongst themselves and claim ownership. Men hold the titles of lands under the laws of the nations. Men dig, plant and reap and call the products of the soil their own. But back of the titles of men, and the claim of nations, God is the great proprietor.

"The earth is the Lord's and the fullness thereof; the world and they that dwell therein" (Psalm 24:1; 1 Corinthians 10:26). "For every beast of the field is Mine, and the cattle upon a thousand hills" (Psalm 50:10-12). "The silver is Mine and the gold is Mine, saith the Lord of hosts" (Haggai 2:8).

Man is a Tenant at the Will of God. — No man really owns the goods in which he deals or the lands to which he holds the deeds. He may be called away from the temporary ownership at any time. It was asked, when a certain very rich man died, "How much did he leave?" The reply was, "He left it all, he took nothing with him." "For we brought nothing into this world, and it is certain we can carry nothing out" (1 Timothy 6:7; Psalm 49:17; Job 1:21). Christ emphasized the uncertain tenure upon which all property is held by the parable of a certain rich man who had much goods laid up, who congratulated himself upon this fact and proposed to pull down his barns and build greater, saying to his soul, "Take thine ease, eat drink and be merry," but God said, "Thou fool, this night thy soul shall be required of thee: then whose shall those things be which thou hast provided" (Luke 12:16-21)?

TRUSTEESHIP

Man as a Trustee. — There is no truth more clearly brought out and stated in many ways in the Bible than that man is in the position of a trustee. Jesus used the parable of the talents to illustrate this great truth (Matthew 25:14-30). It is plainly taught in this parable that man is under obligations to God. No man ever brought himself into the world. No man ever originated his own talent; some men have been endowed with what seems to be greater possibilities than others. To one man has been given the talent for administration, to another that of a ministering spirit, to another mechanical genius, to another that of wealth and to another the power of song or speech. But whatever the talent given, great or small, it is distinctly set forth in the New Testament that it is given in trust and is to be used in the service of Him who has bestowed it.

The business man is expected, by his Lord, to buy and sell, not for himself alone, but as a trustee. In this office it is of great importance that a man be found faithful to the confidence reposed in him (1 Corinthians 4:1,2; Luke 16:2,11; Romans 14:12; Luke 19:11, 27).

A man in a trusteeship, if he is honest, will not waste or squander the property entrusted to his care. He will treat fairly and honestly all men who work for him. The men working for him will feel that they are also trustees seeking to use their skill and time, so that the best interests of God and man may be served.

Man's Right to Hold Property and Do Business is recognized by Christ. In the parable of the pounds (Luke 19:12-26) He commends those who used the money in trading to gain more and were ready when "the nobleman" returned to render a good account. He condemns the man who having received one pound made no effort to increase it. He says, "If ye have not been faithful in the unrighteous mammon, who will commit to your trust the true riches" (Luke 16:11). He made no demand of His disciples, so far as the record shows, to give up their property. The case of the young man of great wealth (Mark 10:17-27), who would follow Christ, and of whom Jesus required that he should divest himself of his property, is fully in accord with Jesus' teaching concerning wealth and the holding of property. The key to the whole matter, on this point, is found in what Jesus says of this very case, "How hard it is for them that trust in riches to enter into the kingdom of God" (Mark 10:24). This young man did not possess his wealth but his wealth possessed him, he was the servant of his money. Jesus' teaching is that a man should hold money in trust. Jesus warned men of the risk of possessing property, lest it become their master. Money, considered simply as money, is a hardening influence and in the restive desire to get more the best things in men are quite sure to be eliminated (Matthew 13:22). "The danger lies in the power of money to gather affection and to absorb trust, thus displacing God" (Matthew 6:19,20,24; Luke 18:24; 12:15).

The Reckoning. — There comes a time when every trustee is called upon to render an account of how he has administered the business entrusted to his care (Matthew 25:19; Luke 19:15). This time may be long delayed, and in the meantime many abuses may grow up, and it may appear that no accounting will ever be demanded; these conditions are plainly pointed out by Jesus in the parables of the vineyard (Luke 20: 9-16) and the tares (Matthew 13:24-30), but it is also made equally clear that in the end every man's work shall be judged.

In this reckoning there can be no making of things appear as they are not. There can be no juggling with the accounts. Every business man must show his books (Revelation 20:12) and how he has dealt with that which was entrusted to his care (1 Corinthians 3:11-15; Romans 2:16; Matthew 25:31-46).

It is the looking forward to the time of reckoning which makes men, who are in offices of earthly trust, pay careful attention to the investment of funds and painstakingly investigate the security offered. Jesus would have every man equally careful in the investment of his time, labour, talent and money for he will surely be called upon to give an account of his stewardship.

In the uncertainty of the time of reckoning every business man is expected to be ready for an investigation at any time when the examiner shall appear (Matthew 24:42-51; Mark 13:34-37; 1 Thessalonians 5:6).

The Profit of business done, as a service in the sight of God, is declared to be sure and large. Whatever sacrifices may have to be made will be more than amply repaid (Matthew 19:27,29; Luke 19: 16-19).

It is a well-known fact that, in the business world at large, there is a very great percentage of failures and too many mark not only wrecks of business, but of characters. The reason often given is that the eye is fixed too frequently and earnestly on immediate and large profits for self. But no man ever yet made a failure who openly and honestly sought in his business to be of service to God and his fellow men. Real failure in business is a failure in character. A business man may be carried down by unexpected circumstances or the fall of other firms but, if he keeps his character intact, he is no failure; on the other hand a man who has taken a selfish advantage of others may be made rich in goods, but he is a rank failure in character. The standard of character in business is after all that by which the small or the large dealer in any kind of goods is judged, and by business men themselves; business transactions are constantly being raised to a higher level by the enforcement of this standard.

PRINCIPLES

If employers and employees are ever to be brought into harmony, strikes and lockouts abolished, the industrial forces attain to their highest efficiency and the products of the world distributed with the utmost facility, it must all come about not by the invoking of courts of law, but by the bringing in of a new sentiment and the adoption of certain principles. A sentiment is at the base of the present troubles and, until it is changed, they will be likely to continue and the world at large will suffer the consequences. So long as men think only of the inequalities of life — and there are glaring inequalities — the unfair distribution of wealth and the comparatively obscure positions which they hold, they will be discontented and will fight to better themselves, no matter who suffers. The spirit of discontent and contention finds lodgment in the heart of the humblest working man, up through all grades, to that of the richest employer, for no man, however wealthy, ever thinks he has enough of this world's goods; those who have the most are often the most eager in grasping for more. Courts of law can only regulate the more flagrant outbursts of the prevailing sentiment, they do not and cannot remedy the causes.

What are some of the principles which are destined to help the industrial world out of its difficulties?

The Observance of the Golden Rule. — "Therefore all things whatsoever ye would that men should do to you, do ye even so to them" (Matthew 7:12). Just before giving this rule Jesus was speaking of a man whose chief object was to serve God (Matthew 6:33) and in the beginning of the Sermon on the Mount, He showed the blessedness of the character which was to be sought (Matthew 5:1-16), before this rule could be rightly carried into practice in any life. "Thou shalt love thy neighbour as thyself" (Matthew 22:39) is in the same line of thought as this rule, but, and here is the point, we do not want certain men to love us as they love themselves, the thief, the gambler, the drunkard, and we do not want them to do to us as they do to themselves.

In order then that this rule be rightly observed there must be first an avowed allegiance to God. "Thou shalt love the Lord thy God" (Matthew 22:37) precedes the command to "Love thy neighbour." It is only when men love God aright and obey His commandments that they can come into proper relations with their neighbours.

Hence, in seeking God first and obeying the Golden Rule, the whole outlook of employer and employee will be changed, the attention will not be fixed upon the inequalities of life or the making of a fortune, but upon the desire to be of service; each man will look into his work to improve it and seek to help his neighbour; whatever the compensation, he will seek to do his best, serving as in the sight of God. "A just consideration of the rights of others is the very beginning and end of true social economy." It is difficult to enforce any law which works against a public sentiment, but let the latter be in favour of the former and the law will enforce itself. Let the sentiment in the industrial business world be in favour of a supreme service and the difficulties and trials of strikes and lockouts would disappear; the energy, time and money now spent in fighting could be turned to the benefit of employer, employee and consumer.

Cooperation. — Jesus never set class over against class. He mingled with the wise and the unwise, the rich and the poor. He sought to draw men together in a common brotherhood; this brotherhood was not composed of employers or of men who worked at a certain trade but of those who sought to build up the kingdom of righteousness.

There is cooperation to-day amongst men but it is the coming together to build up some trade and make it strong that it may contend more stoutly for its rights. There have been various attempts for the federation of unions, but they have too often been for the purpose of coercing a like federation of employers' unions into taking a desired course of action. The world awaits a cooperation of all men in the business world upon the basis of love for each other and seeking for the best interests of all concerned. This again is a sentiment but it is one which must work against the prevailing sentiment of selfishness and looking out for self alone, if ever a better state of things is to be brought about.

The Acceptance of Jesus Christ as the Great Example and Leader.—No man was ever so marvellously endowed with power as Jesus, yet that power was used for the good of mankind. He said "All power is given to Me in heaven and in earth" (Matthew 28:18). He made it a proof of His business on earth that the blind received their sight, the lame walked, the lepers were cleansed, the deaf heard, the dead were raised (Matthew 11:2-6).

The man who follows Christ is the one who makes his business minister to the wants of men and helps them to better conditions, whether he be ruler or ruled.

The glory is that, to-day, there are many men who are trying conscientiously, in the ranks of the employers and employees, to carry out the Golden Rule, cooperate with their fellow men and to follow Christ in His business of ministering to men.

QUESTIONS

What can be said of the ideal in the business world; fight or service? What can be said of the ownership of property? Who is the owner of all? Who is a tenant at the will of God? What can be said of man as a trustee? What can be said of a man's right to hold property? What can be said of the reckoning? What of the profit? What are some of the principles which can help the business world out of its difficulties; the observance of the Golden Rule, cooperation, the acceptance of Jesus Christ as the Great Leader and Example?

STUDY XII

THE CHRISTIAN SOCIETY

Scripture references: Matthew 13:31-33; 5:21-24; Mark 8:1-9; John 2:1-11; Luke 5:29; 14:13; 1 Peter 2:17; Galatians 6:9; Matthew 11:28-30; 12:50; Luke 15:5,6,8-10; John 17:11-15; Luke 5:29,30; Mark 1:28-33; Matthew 6:33; Luke 12:13-15.

THE SOCIAL CIRCLE

The Word Society is used to designate the set of people with whom we are on more intimate terms of acquaintanceship—whom we call friends—and those whom we do not know so well, and whom we call acquaintances. The term society may also have other definitions, such as,

"1. A collective body of persons composing a community, or the aggregate of such communities. 2. A body of persons associated for a common object. 3. The more favoured class or classes, or the fashionable portion of the community."

The Extent of the social circle of any man or woman is largely dependent upon personal choice. There are persons who are exclusive in their preferences and who seek only the society of those of the same rank, wealth or profession as themselves. Hence the different classes in society at large. The pride of the poor often equals the pride of the rich in this matter.

The Character of a social circle is also dependent upon the convictions and opinions of those who compose it. There is a social conscience which is very lax in one group and will allow almost any departure from the moral law, but in another group it is very strict in its requirements. The social conscience is constantly weakened in one case by persons joining the first group, who are weak in moral principle; and as constantly strengthened by those, joining the second group, who are strong in the things which make for a right life.

The Example of Christ. — When Christ came upon earth He found that the rich and educated classes had largely withdrawn from all intercourse with those whom they considered beneath them. He also saw that the tone of society was arrogant and that of moral restraint there was none at all or it was exceedingly weak. The situation was such that many men despaired of anything better and were secluding themselves from intercourse with their fellow men. John the Baptist felt that he could not stem the tide of evil in society and retired to the desert to deliver his message. Those who contend for the regeneration of a corrupt society, and who are decidedly in the minority, always are prone to step outside and seek to do their work there, and sometimes it may be the best to do so.

Jesus however entered into the midst of society. He went to feasts (Luke 5:29,30; 7:36; 19:5). He was present at a wedding (John 2: 1-11). He said that the kingdom of God was like unto ten virgins who prepared to attend a wedding (Matthew 25:1-13). So constantly did He enter into social intercourse with men that the Pharisees and the scribes criticised Him severely for it (Luke 15:2) but Jesus justified His course in being "social to save" by the three parables; the lost sheep, the lost coin and the lost boy (Luke 15:1-24). He gave a great feast at which about five thousand men were present besides women and children (Matthew 14:15-21). He told what garments a guest should wear at a wedding, what seat he should take and who should be invited (Matthew 22:11-14; Luke 14:7-24). He did not wait for men to come to Him, but He went out to meet them by the seaside, and in the city. He sent His disciples out also that He through them might do as wide a work as possible. There is no trace of the recluse in Jesus. He desired to meet people of all classes and mingle with them. At the last He gathered His disciples about Him, in an upper room, and instituted a memorial supper as the chief ordinance of His church (Luke 22:19; Matthew 26:26-30).

Everything that Jesus did in meeting people in a social way had a purpose and that was to level up society and cause it to conform to the principles of the kingdom of God. Wherever He went He led the conversation to the better things of this kingdom. The man who quotes Jesus and His relation to society, as a justification of attendance upon numerous social functions, ought also to carry out the purpose of Jesus in bringing others to a better life; he ought also to lead the conversation to the same topics. If society sways any man from the right purposes of life, and he finds that he cannot breast its temptations he should remain out of it or increase his spiritual strength.

The Christian Society, composed of a body of persons associated for the common object of exploiting Jesus Christ and His principles, at first was almost wholly social. The early Christians met in each others' houses. They partook of meals in common after which they observed the Lord's supper. The basis of organization was the fraternal equality of believers. The barriers between the rich and the poor, the learned and the unlearned, seemed to drop of themselves. No pressure was brought to bear to force men together in this fraternal organization, but they were united by a common love for Jesus Christ, their Lord, and like Him they were at home in all social circles. No law, no urgency of appeal, no pressure, can to-day abolish class distinctions or the conflict between capital and labour. It is only when men's hearts are filled with love for Christ that they cease to antagonize and begin to care for each other and a true social bond is formed.

SOCIAL INSTITUTIONS

"There is no problem of importance to humanity which has not some relation to the Gospel of Christ."

There is a social question and it is a live question. It is closely related to the wrongs and inequalties of life, in wealth, in position, in privileges and in opportunities. There is a social impulse which causes men to get together in smaller and larger groups and through these groups to found institutions which will aid in abolishing the wrongs and in lessening the inequalities. It is in and through social institutions that the larger life of the individual is expressed and he is able to bring about certain results, working in connection with other individuals, which he alone could not bring to pass. In the social organism there is specialization of work, one member performing one function and another another and all working in harmony for a common purpose (1 Corinthians 12:14-27).

There are three great social institutions through which men seek the larger life, the family, the church, and the state. They exist in some form, elementary and crude it may be, wherever man is found.

Christianity entering into all human relations, has much to say about their construction and specific powers and duties. Its mission is not only to regenerate the heart of the individual but to penetrate and transform society. "Its work is to leaven the whole mass of human interests with a divinely purifying power. It touches every act and every relation of humanity with a life from above, and interpenetrates all that a man can do with a new spirit and a heavenly light. It affects governments, moulds education, rectifies manners, sweetens fellowship, makes the common ways of men better, healthier, happier, as well as holier. Its endeavour is to realize a divine society not hereafter only, but upon earth; to have the kingdom of God come not in the skies alone or in the future merely, but here and among men."

The Family. — This is the earliest and most primitive social institution. We are all born into some family, however imperfect its form. Upon the family depends in large measure the good or bad training of the children; here they receive their earliest impressions and what they are taught in the family often dominates all other instruction. If the bond between husband and wife is not regarded as binding and sacred the institution of the family becomes corrupt and a menace to the good order of society.

Jesus spoke in no uncertain way about the sacredness of the marriage relation (Matthew 19:3-9; 5:32) and the obedience which children owed to their parents (Matthew 15:4-6).

The Church. — Man has been called "a religious animal." His desire to worship is instinctive. He seeks the care and protection of a stronger power than himself. Even a man who says he has no religious opinions will often be found, when questioned, to hold most strongly to things which he believes. Individuals, then holding to certain religious beliefs, naturally come together and form groups in which they worship in common. This is the social impulse applied to worship, because man likes to do things in connection with his fellow men.

Christ sought to direct men to the proper object of worship (John 4: 23,24; 14:6-11), the way to pray (Matthew 6:5-15), the way to enter into life with God (John 3:1-21) and the character which was required of those who desired to lead the divine life (Matthew 5:1-16; chapters 5-7). Men who believe in the principles of Jesus Christ associate themselves together in a Christian church.

The Government.—Everywhere we find men uniting for mutual protection against their enemies, the guarding of property, the settling of disputes between individuals, the administration of justice and the exercise of other powers. This government may take different forms from the one man power in a monarchy to that of the most liberal democracy. The necessity for some form of government seems plain.

Christ recognized the duties which a man owed to the state when He said, in answer to the lawyer's question, "Is it lawful to give tribute unto Caesar, or not?" "Render therefore unto Caesar the things which are Caesar's; and unto God the things that are God's." He saw the corruption in the government of His times as plainly as any one, more plainly in fact, but He was showing the necessity of the functions of government. He submitted to the decree of the state condemning Him to death although He knew it to be unjust, and that the power was not with Pilate (John 19:10,11; Matthew 26:52,53).

What Jesus sought to do was to usher in a new kingdom of righteousness. He taught His disciples to pray for the coming of this kingdom upon earth. "Thy kingdom come. Thy will be done in earth as it is in heaven." He was continually speaking of this kingdom (Matthew 13:24-52). He declared that all nations should come to Him finally to be judged (Matthew 25:31,32). One great theme of the prophets of the Old Testament was the righteousness, purity and justice of the new government which God desires to set up amongst men.

Social damage comes to men and great evil is done to individuals when social institutions are not patterned after the plans given by Christ; these are divine institutions when they seek to approach to the divine ideal. Much of the unquiet and restlessness of the masses of men to-day and the great wrongs in the world are due to the tampering with the marriage relation, the substitution of the worship of wealth and worldly power for God, and the seeking of government positions, not to be of service to men under God but to rule over men.

Social health and vigour will come in the family, church and government when men turn again to God and obey and serve Him through the social institutions with supreme love and enthusiasm for His service.

SOCIAL AIMS

In Socialism. — There are many schemes presented to-day under the broad term of Socialism which have for their proposed end the betterment of the people, the abolishment of all wrongs and the bringing in of a new order of things; where every man shall do a minimum amount of work and receive a large return for what he does. These plans vary from the mildest of reforms — and from "the public collective ownership of land and capital and the public collective management of all industries" with the recognition of certain private rights — to the taking of all land and capital absolutely from private control, the abolishing of the right to hold private property, the giving up of the marriage relation, the suppression of the church and the renunciation of the government.

The trouble with extreme schemes of this sort is that they seek in the end to abolish the individual and private rights, even in marriage. But all social and moral health and wealth is but the aggregate of individual health and wealth. No community and no class of men are better than the men who compose them. If there are evils in the present system they would continue, in a magnified form, in the new. There is here the old political fallacy, made over into a new social fallacy, that by mere putting of the ballot into every man's hands the government would be purified of all its evils. We must begin with the individual to purify him before the state or society can be made much better. It is the levelling down, the bringing the better working man to the rate of work and quality of the poorer, which is sought, rather than the levelling up. The common goods scheme was tried early in the career of the Christian Church and it failed to work because of the element of selfishness which came in (Acts 2: 44,45; 4:34; compare 5:1-11); this has been the cause of the breaking up of numerous social and communistic settlements and communities.

In Christianity. — When the precepts of Christianity have been accepted and lived up to by any man or company of men, they have never failed to stand all the social tests which have been applied to them. They seek the regeneration of the individual and the purification and usefulness, for him, of all the social institutions. They endeavour to abolish evil desires and practices in the individual and all social, industrial and political wrongs. They give full play to all man's powers in private and in public matters. They have never been proved inadequate to their task, but they have found much refractory material with which to deal.

They level up not down and seek for every man a new moral and physical life; they present before him the very highest ideals of life and service.

It is a fact that it is only where their light shines that the working man has anything like decent wages or hours of labour. In China, India and Africa we find the labourer gets little or nothing for his toil.

It is only in Christian countries that we have anything approaching true social equality, in others no man may rise out of his caste or class. Take the United States and we find that a number of our presidents have come from the poorest families and most of our influential and wealthy men have risen from the ranks of the common people.

It is the lack of Christian principles in individual, industrial and public life which is at the bottom of the present day social unrest.

In Christ, the Social Reformer. — When He came upon the earth and before His time all labour was performed by slaves without pay and with but a dole of food. The mighty buildings of Egypt, Assyria, Babylonia, Greece and Rome were all built by the unrequited toil of slaves. Such would have continued to be the state of things had not Christ said, "The labourer is worthy of his hire" (Luke 10:7; Matthew 10:10). That a working man should receive wages or any pay for his labour was revolutionary in that time for "Plato, Cicero, Lycurgus held that it was a disgrace to touch the implements of toil." Christ dignified labour by toiling at the bench as a carpenter. If ever labour is to gain any real advantage it must be through taking Christ as a leader (Matthew 11:28).

He taught that the true bond of social equality was a moral and spiritual one (Luke 8:21; Matthew 23:8; Philippians 3:13-15; 4:8).

In the Social Settlement.—What is a true social settlement? This question is not so easily answered. There are all kinds and sorts of social settlements. Some minister to the health of the community in which they are situated and some do not. The saloon has recently put forth its claim to the doing of social service, but no one ever slandered a saloon keeper by affirming that he had anything in view save a selfish motive. Whatever little social service he may render is more than counterbalanced by the social havoc wrought by his trade. Again there are social settlements where the principal thought and effort seems to be to provide somewhat questionable vaudeville entertainments and frequent public dances; the leaders say they are compelled to adopt these features to hold the people; here comes in again the question of social damage to the community in which they are situated.

The true social settlement, with all its features of mental and physical culture, is one which places Christ at the front of all its work and keeps Him there. It is Christ and Christ alone who can really help the individual and the community and there are numbers of social settlements where Christ is kept at the head of the work.

The church has changed its methods very much during the past few years. Seldom is a church now built which does not have its well appointed kitchen, dining-room and parlours and other social equipments. It is according as a church uses these adjuncts, whether they really help it, or not, to do its work. The church is powerful as a force for social betterment not as it does or does not open its doors to lecturers, plan social entertainments, give dinners and hold festivals—these may be helps—but in so far as it sways the inner life of the community. This inner life, influenced in right ways, finds expression in a better individual, home and community standard. This standard makes for the uplifting of the social state outside as well as inside the church. The principle is, not social for the sake of being social, but "social to save." It is quite certain that unless the church sets up its ideals in the community, a worldly community will set up its ideals in the church. The more spiritual a church as a social settlement is the stronger the social bond becomes between rich and poor, the learned and the unlearned.

BROTHERHOOD

The Christian Social Brotherhood is not a brotherhood of a class but of all classes and conditions of men. To-day the popular idea of brotherhood is the association of men of a certain trade. There is a strong tendency for social groups to be formed, which are exclusive of all who do not conform to a certain standard in the industrial world and inclusive of all who do. The members are looking for protection and mutual benefit.

Christ said of His brotherhood, "One is your Master, even Christ and all ye are brethren…. One is your Father which is in heaven" (Matthew 23:8,9). We find here the great principle laid down that there can be no true brotherhood without a common fatherhood. Christians are brothers because they have a common "Master" and "Father" hence they seek to do good not only to the members of the brotherhood but to all men, because God is the Father of all. It is this thought that is to bring men up out of their selfishness. The employer and employee will strive to do all they can for each other when deep down in their hearts they believe they are brethren in Christ; we shall hear no more then of injustice upon either side.

The church of Jesus Christ holds the only solution to the peaceful and happy settlement of the social unrest.

QUESTIONS

What can be said of the social circle, what does the word society signify? What is the extent of any social circle, the character? What can be said of the example of Christ in society, the Christian society? What can be said of social institutions; the family, the church, the government? What can be said of social aims; Socialism, Christianity, Christ, the social reformer, the church as a social settlement? What can be said of the Christian social brotherhood?

STUDY XIII

THE CHRISTIAN STATE

Scripture references: Matthew 22:17-22; 17:24-27; Acts 23:5; John 6:15; Matthew 4:8-10; John 18:36-38; Mark 14; 61,62; John 18:33; 19:19; Isaiah 9:6,7; 60:3; Zechariah 9:10; Daniel 7:14; Matthew 26:64; 26:53,54; 16:16,17; 25:31,32.

CHRIST AND THE STATE

The Relation of Christ to the State.—He was an intense patriot. He loved His country. The names of His great countrymen, Abraham, Isaac, Jacob, Joshua and David, were ever on His lips. He offered Himself as the national Messiah (Matthew 21:1-17), He was rejected (John 18:38-19:16; Luke 23:27-30; 13:34) and crucified (John 19:18), after He had been unjustly condemned to death both by the Jewish and Roman authorities. Upon the cross and over His head was placed the inscription, "Jesus of Nazareth the King of the Jews."

What Jesus Taught About the State.—The ancient idea of the state was that it was everything and the individual nothing. The first question was, "Is the state strong and prosperous?" The happiness or unhappiness of the individual was not considered. The purity or impurity of the life of the individual was of little consequence. The citizens existed for the state and to serve it and its ruler. This idea has lingered long and is not entirely yet extinct.

1. Jesus discovered the individual in the state. He taught that the soul of one man is worth more than the whole world (Matthew 16:26). Jesus put the individual first and the state second. This teaching was entirely new and revolutionary. Christ's principle was make the man, the unit, right and the state will be right. He insisted that the test of the state is the kind of individuals it produces (Matthew 7:16). "By their fruits ye shall know them" (Matthew 7:20). Formerly the state was thought of as an institution to minister to the

comfort or happiness of the ruler or ruling class. Christ reversed this when He declared that rulers existed to serve the state. He said, "Ye know that the princes of the Gentiles exercise dominion over them, and they that are great exercise authority upon them. But it shall not be so among you, but whosoever will be great among you let him be your minister; and whosoever will be chief among you let him be your servant. Even as the Son of Man came not to be ministered unto, but to minister and to give His life a ransom for many" (Matthew 20: 25-28). He is the greatest in the state who renders the greatest service.

2. "He laid the foundation of a true state." In the time of Christ the common people had no choice in the selection or election of any officer of the state, of high or low position. Popular government in any form was unknown. If things went wrong people must endure them. When Jesus laid the responsibility upon the individual He made a basis for a popular government of some form. If things are not right now in a Christian state the people have the power of protest and change. It is for the people to send their representatives to the legislature, to congress, to parliament, etc., and to make and alter the laws when new laws or changes are needed.

3. He was a civil reformer from the inside. Jesus taught the necessity for the moral and spiritual regeneration of men before much could be done by the state in weeding out its evils. He saw plainly the folly of trying to transform the character of the state solely by the coercive power of law. "Satan tempted Him to take the short cut,—seize power over men and then change the character in men (Matthew 4:8). To have become the kind of a king the Galileans proposed in John 6:15 would have frustrated His mission. He sought in society and politics what He sought in each man's life (Matthew 12:36; 23:26; Luke 6:45; John 10:10). Jesus was a true reformer."

4. Jesus taught obedience to the state and Himself strictly observed what He taught. He paid His taxes (Matthew 17:24-27). He declared that it was lawful to give tribute to Caesar (Matthew 22:15-21). When He was unlawfully arrested, on a trumped up charge, He made no resistance (John 18:1-9); this was not because He was not able to do so, for He could have summoned more than twelve le-

gions of angels to aid Him (Matthew 26:53). Jesus thoroughly understood the corruption of His times, and the character of the rulers. He said of Herod, when it was told Him that he would kill Him, "Go ye and tell that fox, Behold, I cast out devils and do cures today and to-morrow, and the third day I shall be perfected" (Luke 13:32,33). He obeyed the law for a purpose and the bringing in of a new order of things—the abolition of force and the substitution for it of service in the kingdom of God. He suffered the Just for the unjust. He was a Martyr for His country. He died that it might live in a new order of men, under the banner of Christianity.

5. He taught the right principles upon which the universal state should be founded. Up to and at the time of Christ nations were separated from each other not only by natural boundaries of rivers, seas, plains, mountains, languages and racial differences but by religions. One people worshipped one set of gods, while another people bowed down to other gods. Jesus set forth the large ideal of uniting all races and all peoples in one great spiritual kingdom (John 18:37; Matthew 28:19,20; Acts 1:8; 17:24-27). It is only as different peoples and nations are united in a common religion that there can be a proper political federation or union (John 4:20-24; 10:16). Jesus taught His disciples to pray that God's kingdom, a reign of righteousness, justice and peace, might come, not to one people only, but to all peoples. This prayer, "Thy kingdom come. Thy will be done in earth as it is done in heaven" (Matthew 6:10) means that the earth and no one restricted part of it is to be occupied by the kingdom of God. Jesus looked beyond the Jewish state and the Roman state and saw the beginning of a kingdom of God which would embrace all nations. It is this kingdom which is to permeate, purify and control the governments of the earth.

THE AUTHORITY

The Source of Authority is in God. "There is no power but of God; the powers that be are ordained of God" (Romans 13:1; Daniel 2:20,21; 4:32; Psalm 2). God is sovereign. He is the final basis of all authority. "Government has authority delegated to do its duties, but it has no inherent authority to do anything. God has inherent powers; institutions have that which is conferred upon them by law.

Each one who exercises authority must derive it directly or indirectly from God" (Matthew 18:18; Daniel 7:13,14; Isaiah 9:6,7; Luke 10:22; John 3:35). This is one of the fundamental principles of the Christian state. This authority may be delegated to men and may be used rightly or it may be abused.

In the Old and New Testaments it is distinctly taught that all nations — Christian and unchristian — are directly accountable to God.

The Sanction of Authority is in the righteousness and justice of God. "Shall not the Judge of all the earth do right" (Genesis 18:25; Psalm 58:11; 67:7; 97:6; 9:8; 50:6; Proverbs 16:11,12; Romans 3:21,22)? The Old Testament prophets looked forward to the perfect state wherein righteousness and justice should rule. Sovereignty over a state may be initiated by force but it can never be made the permanent basis on which sovereignty rests. "States have been defrauded of their birthright with scarcely the grace of a contract for a mess of pottage, but the possession may be kept only by a return to justice. The strongest is not strong enough to be always master, unless he transform his strength into right and obedience to duty."

THE LAW

Reign of Law. — The philosopher, the natural scientist and the Christian theologian all believe that we live in a universe governed by law. Certain natural scientists may believe that the law is impersonal in its origin, but the Christian theologian believes that the origin of law, and the carrying it out, is "the expression of the will of a personal God."

Law has been defined, as the necessary relations which pertain to the nature of things. When men come to associate themselves in a state they find it necessary to define and formally set forth their relations by certain enactments for the general good, which are called laws. But these laws naturally will be the expression of, and will rise no higher than, the social conscience of the people.

The revealed will of God in regard to men and their political relations to each other, as given in the Scriptures, presents high ideals, which, if realized, go to make the perfect state (Micah 6:8). The Old

Testament prophets were continually presenting these divine ideals of the state to the people of Israel and urging them to accept them. Christ had much to say about the higher political relations of men. Paul in his epistles also had much to say upon this topic. Moses urged not only the keeping of the provisions of the ceremonial, but also the moral and civil laws (Deuteronomy 6:1-9; Exodus 25:40; Joshua 1:7; Exodus 13:9; Nehemiah 9:13; Psalm 1:2; Isaiah 1:10-17; Jeremiah 8:7,8; Daniel 9:10,11; Matthew 5:17; 22:36-40; Hebrews 8:10; Titus 3:1,2; Ezra 7:25).

God is the Lord of all nations and they are to be judged according to His law (Psalm 2; 47:2,3; Malachi 1:14; Psalm 67:4; Matthew 28:19; 25:32; Romans 16:26).

The End of the Law is to make a holy nation, wherein righteousness shall reign. The effort of the Mosaic law was to make Israel a "holy nation." Even sanitary and dietary laws were not laid down as such but were made the distinctive marks of the consecrated life of a chosen people; details of ritual were prescribed to express the sense of the holiness of God in whose service they were exercised (Exodus 19:6). "And ye shall be holy unto Me; for I the Lord am holy, and have severed you from other people, that ye should be Mine" (Leviticus 20:26; Deuteronomy 7:6; 26:19; 28:9; Isaiah 62:12; 1 Corinthians 3:17).

The effort of Christianity, under the leadership of Christ, is not only to perfect the church, but also the state. In so far as the principles of Christianity prevail amongst the people they reflect themselves in the laws of the state. In a community which is thoroughly Christian it is impossible for certain evil institutions to maintain themselves.

The Duty of the Christian Citizen is to recognize the state, to give it loyal support and obedience and to seek to make its law conform to the law ordained by God. No man ought to hold himself aloof from the political interests of his community or country. In many towns and cities where Christian public sentiment has secured the passage of excellent laws for the suppression of certain evils, the evils flourish in spite of the good laws because they are not strongly supported by that sentiment which secured their passage.

Never was there a time when the highest type of Christian citizenship, setting forth the ideals of Christ, was more needed than at the present day. The outlook for any true national greatness must necessarily be from an ethical and Christian standpoint, bringing to the front the principles of love, loyalty, service and sacrifice.

FUNCTIONS AND PURPOSE

Functions.—The Christian state is continually widening its sphere of care and action over and for the individual. It not only assumes the protection of life and property, but provides schools, from the primary grade to great universities; it cares for the sick and mentally deficient; it provides food, clothing and shelter for the destitute poor, it supervises the morals of the people, and enforces sanitary regulations. The more thoroughly Christian the state the more it seeks the betterment of the individual. The less Christian the state the less it cares for the good of the individual and the more it seeks to oppress and to use him as its slave.

Purpose—This is the realization of the kingdom of God on earth. The Christian is working for a state, where the principles of justice and brotherly love shall prevail.

QUESTIONS

Christ and the state; what was His relation to the state? What did He teach about the state? What did Jesus teach about the individual and his relation to the state? In what way did He lay the foundation of the true state? In what respect was He a civil reformer? What did Jesus teach about obedience to the state? What did He teach about the universal state and the principles upon which it should be founded? What is the source of authority for the state? Give the sanction of its authority. What can be said of the law of the state, the reign of law, definition, end of the law and the duty of the Christian citizen? Give the functions and purpose of the Christian state.

STUDY XIV

THE CHRISTIAN'S HOPE

Scripture references: 1 Timothy 1:1; Colossians 1:27; Psalm 130:5; 43:5; Proverbs 10:8; Acts 24:15; Psalm 71:5; Romans 5:1-5; 12:12; 15:4; 1 Corinthians 9:10; Galatians 5:5; Ephesians 1:18; Philippians 1:20; Colossians 1:5; 1 Thessalonians 1:3; 2:19; Titus 1:2; 2:13; 3:7; Psalm 31:24; 71:14,15.

HOPE IN THE PRESENT LIFE

That which a man ardently hopes for he strives to realize. If he desires fame, office or wealth he will seek to set forces in motion, here and now, which will bring him that which his soul covets. Back of every man's striving there is always some hope, an ideal, which he endeavours to make a reality.

The man who enthusiastically believes in Jesus Christ cherishes the hope that every man may be brought to believe in his Lord and Master (Acts 26:27-29). He wants to see Christ not only rule and reign in the life to come, but in this present life.

The urgency of the New Testament appeals to men is to, at once, believe in Jesus Christ, and to begin to live the Christian life (Acts 16:31-33; 2 Corinthians 6:1-10; Galatians 2:20). The attempt was made by the early preachers of Christianity to bring about upon the earth a new order of things. They prayed and laboured for the immediate conversion of men's souls and the betterment of the conditions under which men lived. A new kingdom (Matthew 10:32-42; Mark 1:14,15) was inaugurated with new ideals (Matthew 5:1-16), new principles and new aspirations, which was to supersede the old social and political orders. It was the preaching of this kingdom of Christ, and that men owed their first allegiance to it (Acts 5:28,29), which provoked the terrible persecutions of the first centuries.

Christianity has much to do with this present life, it has a panacea for all its ills and evils and it has a certain definite programme to carry out.

The Christian hopes and works for:

The Regeneration of the Individual through faith in Christ (John 3:5,14-21). This is an inward change wrought in the soul by the grace of God. While this is a work of God, the responsibility for it rests with man. God does not desire the death of the sinner. By the sending of Jesus Christ God has shown His love for man while yet a sinner. Every unregenerate man either does not desire this new life or else feels that he never sought with all his heart to have God regenerate his soul (John 5:40; 1:4; 5:24; Isaiah 1:18). The regenerate man in Christ thinks and acts from a new basis (2 Corinthians 5:17; Galatians 6:15). It is only as the love of a man's heart is really changed and centred upon right things that he can be depended upon to walk in right ways. A man may act right, may be honest and upright from prudential motives, but if his heart is evil the way of the righteous will be irksome to him and he may depart from it at any time. The unmasking of the double life of a man, every now and then, shows how the heart's desire will have its way with a man who does not love God. Heart faith in Christ leads a man to follow and be like Him.

Hence we have such a large emphasis placed upon work for and with the individual by Christ and His disciples. Christ Himself called His apostles to Him one by one and He was continually holding conversations of the deepest interest with individuals (John 3:1-13; 4:6-26).

The possibilities of the work of the individual Christian for the individual non-Christian man are too largely left untried. If every follower of Christ should try to win one, who did not follow Him, to His cause every year the good effects of such a campaign would be felt not only in the church, but in every department of life.

All true reform work must begin with the regeneration of the individual.

The Enlightenment of the Social Conscience.—There is such a thing as a social conscience. It is possible to say and do things in certain communities which would not be tolerated in others. One town will not only sanction the liquor business within its boundaries but will resist all efforts to abolish it; another town right beside it will have none of this iniquitous traffic. Lawlessness and immorality find a hearty welcome in certain cities and in others they dare not show themselves. All this is due not to the perfection or the imperfection of the laws or to the large number or small number of men upon the police force, but to an evil, an apathetic or an enlightened social conscience.

The progress of the gospel of Christ is often hindered or prevented by a hostile public sentiment (Matthew 13:58; 17:20; 10:14; Luke 10:10-12). When Christ sent forth His twelve disciples He recognized the strong opposition which their message and mission would often meet and said, "Behold, I send you forth as sheep in the midst of wolves; be ye therefore wise as serpents and harmless as doves" (Matthew 10:16). The disciples were taught to expect social ostracism and private and public persecution (Matthew 10:17-26). There were times when they were to flee before the gathering storm of opposition and there were times in which they were to maintain their position to the death, but even if they fled (Matthew 10:23) they were not to cease to preach the gospel.

It is the duty and the right of Christians not only to seek for the regeneration of individuals, but also to protest and work against social and political wrongs and to seek to create and strengthen a strong public Christian sentiment. The Church of Christ should be the conservator and promoter of high moral ideals in every city and town where it has a name and place and seek to extend its good influence into regions where it has no standing.

Better Conditions of Living. — The Bible is always upon the side of the oppressed and down-trodden. No laws ever enacted by any nation ever made it so easy for the working man as the Mosaic ordinances; every seventh day (Exodus 20:9,10) was a day of rest; there were seven feasts in seven months which called for many other days of rest; every seventh year (Leviticus 25:2-7) was a rest year; and every fiftieth year (Leviticus 25:10-17) was one of rest and restitution. Christ everywhere championed the cause of the poor and the heavy burdened (Matthew 9:36; 11:28-30; 11:4,5).

But the Bible also clearly sets forth the fact that little can be done towards bettering even the material conditions of living when men's hearts are not right towards God. If a man lets the spirit of avarice reign over him, no matter how much money he may have he will still want more and he will not care whom he oppresses to get it. If the spirit of a purely worldly pleasure rules him his money will go into a bottomless pit and he will not care whom he makes suffer to get more money to gratify his insatiable desires.

Better material conditions of work and living can only come from the adoption of high moral and spiritual standards and in advocating these the Christian Church to-day is the truest friend of the oppressed.

The Maintenance of Law and Order. — It is not an unusual thing for political parties to elect men to offices of trust and then to have these same men refuse to enforce the laws which they have sworn to uphold. In consequence we have all kinds of abuses and evils growing up in the body politic. Too often the political race is for the honour and the spoils of position.

Outside the political arena stands the Christian Church and it can, if it will, demand that clean and upright men, whatever the issues of the parties may be, be placed in nomination. Here Christians may hold the balance of power. If their loyalty is to Christ first of all they will vote for no man for any office who is known to be of an evil character. The maintenance of law and order depends in large measure, in any community, upon the Christian sentiment of that community.

The Turning of the World to Christ. — The Christian's hope is that Christ may be Lord of and dominate the individual and the home life, the social, the business and the political worlds, as well as the ecclesiastical.

The worship of God in Christ ought not to be only upon a particular day or in a certain place, but upon all days and in every place men should lift up their hearts to Him (John 4:21-24). If He is Lord of all (John 1:1-14; 14:9-13) He should be Lord of all; there is no matter too small and none too great to bring before Him. When Christ said, "Go ye therefore and teach all nations ... teaching them to observe all things whatsoever I have commanded you" (Matthew

28:19,20) He meant that His teachings should be dominant over all the earth and in every department of life. And for this we pray "Thy Kingdom come, Thy will be done in earth as it is in heaven" (Matthew 6:10). It is only as this kingdom shall come in power that we can expect to better the conditions under which men live and work.

HOPE IN THE FUTURE LIFE

Christianity is not small in its anticipations, its desires, its aspirations and its plans.

It speaks of a large hope for the future, so large that many men fail to comprehend its magnificence (John 11:23-26; Mark 16:11). It declares that while the body may be placed in the grave, the real man never dies. Man in all that he thinks and does lives with two worlds plainly in view, the one that now is and the one which is to come.

The disciples immediately after the ascension of Christ began to preach and teach the resurrection from the dead (Acts 2:30-32; 3:15; 4:10,33; 1 Corinthians 15:1-8). They used this fact of the resurrection as a reason for the belief in Christ as the Saviour of men, a forsaking of sin and an incentive to a life of righteousness. They taught, as Jesus Himself did, that this life, no matter how great its opportunities, was but the vestibule to a new and larger life beyond the grave. It is better to sacrifice everything in this life, if necessary, rather than to miss the glory of the life to come (Matthew 5:29; 10:28; Mark 9:47). No good deed done in this life, in the name of Christ, can fail of large reward in the life to come (Matthew 19:28,29; 25:34-40). By this emphasis, which was laid upon the future life, the horizon of thought and action was marvellously widened. Men were taught no longer that they were to exist for a few years and then go out forever into the darkness of annihilation, good and bad alike, but that they were to live forever.

Conscious Personal Existence of the soul after death. This fact is conspicuously taught in the Gospels, the Acts, the Epistles and Revelation. In the world to come people are not shades or ghosts, but they have certain bodies (1 Corinthians 15:44), they know themselves to be and are known as the same persons who once lived on the earth (Matthew 17:2-4; Luke 24:36-48; John 20:24-28; 11:25,26; Luke 16:19-31; 23:42,43). Christ said, "But as touching the resurrection of the dead have ye not read, that which was spoken unto you by God saying, I am the God of Abraham, the God of Isaac, and the God of Jacob? God is not the God of the dead, but the living" (Matthew 22: 31,32).

Eternal Citizenship in heaven. The aim of Christianity is to make men righteous. The abode of the blessed hereafter is one wherein dwells holiness, purity and truth.

There are conditions and hindrances to the entering of the abode of the blessed.

1. Conditions. The great prerequisite to entering into the joy of heaven is righteousness, perfect obedience to the law of God. But every man of himself, when he enters into an honest self-examination, feels that he comes far short of the perfect keeping of the divine commands (1 John 1:8,9; Romans 3:23). He needs forgiveness for past disobedience, he needs help to lead a righteous life. Hence Jesus Christ, the divine Son of God, came that through His life and death we might receive pardon for past sin and help to live the righteous life (John 3:16-23). What man could not do for himself Jesus Christ does for him (Romans 3:20-26). The disciples of Christ were rightly enthusiastic in proclaiming Him as the propitiation for man's sin and belief in Him, with all that it implied, as the entrance gate into the heavenly life. Jesus said of Himself, "I am the way, the truth and the life; no man cometh unto the Father but by Me" (John 14:6). "In My Father's house are many mansions if it were not so I would have told you. I go to prepare a place for you. And if I go and prepare a place for you, I will come again and receive you unto Myself; that where I am, there ye may be also" (John 14:2,3).

2. Hindrances. The great hindrance to the entering of heaven is disobedience of God, not only acts of disobedience but a state of disobedience, where the soul of man desires to have no fellowship with God or His righteousness. There is a disobedience of God through carelessness, through ignorance and through willfulness; there is little hope for a man when he deliberately turns his back upon God. It is wonderfully shown in the Bible how God has sought to make Himself known to man and to save him here and

hereafter. Every possible appeal has been made to man to turn to God. The Scriptures give no answer of hope for a happy hereafter for those who deliberately reject all of God's invitations and pleadings in this world (Matthew 25:46; Daniel 12:2; John 5:29; Romans 2:1-6).

The Glory of Heaven. — The New Testament writers vie with each other in striving to make plain the glory of heaven. John describes it, in a vision, as a magnificent city of gold and precious stones, wherein can come no evil thing (Revelation, chapters 21,22). "And the city had no need of the sun, neither of the moon, to shine in it: for the glory of God did lighten it, and the Lamb is the light thereof. And the nations of them which are saved shall walk in the light of it: and the kings of the earth do bring their honour and glory into it" (Revelation 21:23,24). The real glory of heaven, however, is not in its outward adornment or pageantry, but in the triumph of righteousness and the supreme reward of constancy to the truth of God (Revelation 7:9-17). The holiness of God is vindicated (Revelation 4:8,9). "The tabernacle of God is with men" (Revelation 21:3,4), and every good deed stands out glorified in the clear white light of eternity. Every saint in heaven will feel that he has the hundredfold reward for all the sacrifices he made when upon the earth for the kingdom of God.

The effort of the New Testament writers is to make the followers of Christ joyfully do their work here, much of which may be distasteful and difficult. "Looking unto Jesus the author and finisher of our faith; who for the joy that was set before Him endured the cross, despising the shame and is set down at the right hand of the throne of God" (Hebrews 12:2). It is worth while to work for a limited future earthly reward; it is much more worth while to work for a heavenly reward which shall endure throughout eternity.

QUESTIONS

What can be said of the Christian's hope in the present life? What is the regeneration of the individual through faith in Christ? What is meant by the enlightenment of the social conscience? How can better conditions of living be secured through Christ? How can law and order be maintained through the advancement of Christian principles? What is the Christian's hope in turning the world to Christ? What is the Christian's hope in the future life? What is meant by conscious personal existence after death, eternal citizenship, the glory of heaven?